Heretics, Mystics & Misfits

*A collection of sermons on the famous
and infamous in the history of Christianity*

JOHN R. MABRY

For Liz

Many blessings!

apocryphile press
BERKELEY, CA

apocryphile press
BERKELEY, CA

Apocryphile Press
1700 Shattuck Ave #81
Berkeley, CA 94709
www.apocryphile.org

This book of sermons is dedicated to
the people of Grace North Church,
for whom they were written,
my spiritual family for nearly
ten years;

and especially to Robert DeVelbiss,
who enjoyed them so.

Also by John R. Mabry

God As Nature Sees God:
A Christian Reading of the Tao Te Ching

The Little Book of the Tao Te Ching

Contents

Apologies
& Acknowledgements

The sermons in this collection were preached over a four-year period at the parish where I am privileged to serve as co-pastor, Grace North Church in Berkeley, California. It is the custom in our parish to diverge from the lectionary each summer for a "course" on various subjects. Two courses are presented here, the first on a survey of Christian heresy, and the second on medieval and post-enlightenment mystics.

I am very grateful to the congregation at Grace North for their encouragement of these series over the years. I cannot imagine a more supportive environment. Any preacher that can stand up in his pulpit and say, "I am a heretic" or "I do not believe in God" without reprisal (both of which I have done) has found a very special congregation indeed. Certainly, not everyone has appreciated every sermon, but the caring feedback I have received over the years has made me a better preacher, and I hope, a better pastor as well.

One complaint that was made several years ago is the focus on my fundamentalist past as a starting place for sermons. I have taken this critique to heart, and although I still occasionally begin a sermon with a contrasting story from my religious upbringing, I am more cautious about this than I was in the past. This practice is on full display in this collection, unfortunately. Fully 50% of the sermons that follow begin with a story from my fundamentalist past. One can always tell what a preacher is dealing with from the content of his or her sermons. It has been said that preachers are always ultimately preaching to themselves, and in my experience this is certainly true. The careful reader will see that the introductions to many sermons, as well as the subject of the series' themselves, are evidence of the very hard work I have been doing to heal from the religious abuse of my formative years. I apologize to the reader for this fundie-centric approach, and I hope that the careful working out of my own salvation on display will provide another layer of meaning for the reader to enjoy rather than an annoyance to be borne.

I want to thank Dr. Janeen Jones for her careful proofreading, suggestions, and enthusiastic encouragement. I also want to acknowledge the many wonderful sources from which the material in this collection is drawn, especially David Christie-Murray's excellent *A History of Heresy*, which was absolutely essential to the initial series. Great thanks also to the entire run of *Gnosis* magazine, which I consulted more than I can possibly account for. Other sources are acknowledged in the bibliography. I apologize for any volumes I have inadvertently omitted. Also, I have endeavored at every turn to make my words my own. If anyone discovers a sentence or two that bears too close a resemblance to any in my source materials, I beg the reader to bring this to my attention so that I may correct subsequent editions.

Lastly, as a feminist, I am committed to inclusivity in theory, if not always in practice. Our parish is progressive theologically, but I fear, quite conservative liturgically. We might be heretical in our message, but the language of our prayer is still the 1662 *Book of Common Prayer*, and the Jacobean cadences, militant metaphors, and sexist language are still in full force in our community. This has caused me a great deal of discomfort, but I have, after ten years in the pulpit of this parish, become more or less resigned to this reality. I have tried to correct such language for this edition, and I beg the reader's forbearance for any occasional lapse in inclusivity that might be found.

In spite of its myriad and sundry shortcomings, I hope that readers can overlook this volume's warts and enjoy the journey offered. It has been a great deal of fun for me and, I think, for our parishioners as well. Enjoy.

John R. Mabry
Alameda, CA

Introduction:
The Faith of Our Fathers?

Several years ago I went through a huge crisis of faith, a crisis from which I emerged a different sort of animal. It was part of a transformation that had actually been taking place for the past ten years, and yet for the life of me I could not admit to myself what had happened. I managed to stay in denial for a long time, but I was finally brought to my knees by some research. It astounded me, and I found that in the end, I simply had to come out of the closet and admit to the world that "I am a heretic."

I did not come to this realization lightly. I fought it long and hard. It felt like it would kill me to finally admit to myself that I was not, after all, an orthodox Christian.

In fact, I made some herculean efforts to try to maintain my self image as one. My sermon series on the Apostles Creed in the summer of 1997 was a last ditch attempt on my part to claim the label "orthodox" for myself; to find some way to reconcile the Creed with what I actually believe about God, humanity, and the universe. But I am relieved, now, at last, to let go of these efforts, and simply let what is, be.

I doubt this revelation will come as much of a shock to those of you who are familiar with my sermons and other writings. But you will perhaps also understand why it was so difficult for me to admit it to myself.

You see, I grew up in an extremely conservative religious tradition that enjoyed talking about Hell much more than was healthy for anybody involved. I heard sermons on hellfire from before I was old enough to speak, so the terror of damnation, of God's rejection, is a primal fear that looms large in my psyche.

To admit to myself, to God, and to you that I can in no way consider myself an orthodox Christian is a very scary thing, for it means that I can no longer claim the salvation of the orthodox God. A part of me feels that by admitting this to myself, to actually say it aloud, I have consigned myself to the very hellfire that caused me to tremble as a little boy. To lots of orthodox Christians, it means that I am an outcast, that God has rejected me; some of them may say that I have become a bad person, even an evil person.

But I reject such small-hearted, sweeping damnations. It is my sincere belief, and the testimony of history, that heretics are *not* evil people. Throughout the last two thousand years, those whom the orthodox have consigned to the outer darkness have been, in fact, most sincere and heart-felt believers.

For much of the church's history, heretics have stood firm in their faith even though it meant imprisonment, torture, or execution. Theirs is a faith bought hard, with their own blood. Did they go to their graves because they were evil people? I think it more likely that they went because they were honest people. They were people of integrity, who could not compromise their faith just to be in sync with the majority.

Did God judge these people as harshly as the church has? None of us can know. It is my guess, however, that God is much more pleased with a person who genuinely wrestles with his or her faith and comes to an erroneous conclusion, than God is with someone who simply follows blindly whatever faith they were given as children, even if it happens to be correct.

One thing I do know is that, as a heretic, I am in very good company. Almost every one of our greatest heroes of faith started out their careers as heretics. Jesus was murdered for his heresy. The Buddha is still today considered a heretic by orthodox Hindus. Ask Martin Luther what it felt like to be a heretic, for surely he was one, or George Fox, the founder of the Quakers. Any person who has ever held out for what the Holy Spirit was whispering in their secret heart over dogma knows this struggle. Perhaps you, dear reader, know it, too.

The truly sad part is that the orthodox Christians themselves were considered heretics by the earliest Christian church in Jerusalem. Paul was known not as "The Apostle" but "Paul the Apostate" and anyone belonging to one of the churches he helped to found was considered a heretic. But as the Pauline church grew in number, the tables were turned. Those who followed the original teachings of Jesus were, in the end, despised as heretics, as those who followed the religion invented by Paul declared themselves to be the orthodox guardians of the faith.

While it seems shocking to some people, there were more than two kinds of Christianity in the early church. In addition to the Jerusalem church and the Pauline church, there were other groups who held still different understandings of what it means to follow Jesus. As one historian has put it, we cannot speak about "early Christianity" as such; we must speak of "early Christianities" in the plural, because it wasn't until the large church councils in the third century that the dogmas became written in stone, putting an end to the amazing diversity of theologies.

I think there are just as many "Christianities" today. None of us believe exactly the same things. Even if we use the same words to describe our faith, the pictures in our heads look very different indeed. The old saying that "where you have two Jews you have three opinions" holds true for Christians as well; we're just not quite as honest as Jews are about such things.

I believe this is because in Christianity we define our membership in the group by "what we believe" while Jews are Jews because they are born into the family. No matter what their opinions, even if they are athiests, they are still Jews.

I feel kind of cheated by Christianity for this reason. It seems to me that the spiritual life is a long one, with many unexpected twists and turns. We need to have a place where we can encourage each other to follow the inner urgings of the spirit, to support each other as we struggle from one understanding to the next. Instead, most Christians do not support this journey, for if God should lead one out of the "correct opinions" they are most likely reviled and shunned, if not outright excommunicated.

The tragedy is that this person may in another year or two have grown in many areas of his or her life, and be led again into more "acceptable" opinions, but by this time the community has turned its back on him or her.

This is not, I think, how Jesus would have wanted it. Jesus was never concerned with making sure people regurgitated the correct dogma. Jesus was always much more concerned about people feeling loved by God. Intellectual assent to a set of propositions was not among Jesus' criteria of who was acceptable. Scripture tells us that once Jesus' disciples came to tattle on those using his name to minister, even though they were "not one of us!" Jesus responded with great generosity of heart. He didn't say "Oh my gosh! We have to tell them to stop it!" Nor did he insist anyone be executed for having the nerve to do something so terrible as healing the sick. Instead, he said something much more shocking. He said, "Leave them alone. Anyone who is not against us is for us."

This was a much more humane response, I believe. Similarly, I think it is possible for us to find a more humane, even, if you will, a more authentically Christian response to each others' journeys, even when they seem to lead into strange valleys. My own personal opinion is that anyone who sincerely strives to follow Jesus to the best of his or her understanding and ability has the right to call themselves a "Christian." I invite you to consider this definition for yourself. You may find that you are a Christian after all!

Now you may be thinking, "Wait a minute, aren't some heresies dangerous?" Of course. There are some heresies which should be rejected, but only after being given a fair hearing.

This is more than many heart-felt believers received from the orthodox. As we shall see in chapter seventeen, Peter Servitus, the founder of modern Universalism, fled persecution during the reformation, and sought out John Calvin, sure that Calvin would listen to him and help him and his congregation endure. But when Servitus finally reached Geneva, not only did Calvin not support him, but he ordered him burned at the stake. Calvin himself lit the match.

The time for burning is over. It is instead, I believe, time to take a close look, perhaps for the first time ever, at what Servitus and so many others who were inhumanely punished were actually punished for.

It probably will not surprise you that some people were declared heretics for reasons more political than theological, or that the resulting theology often became unbalanced when competing truths could not be held in tension, but this is precisely what has happened time and again in the history of the church.

Which voices were silenced, and rightfully so? Which voices were silenced that should not have been, leaving the church theologically impoverished? In the following pages we will explore these questions together, recounting the tale of the shaping of the Christian church—only this time, we will listen to those who were never given a fair hearing. If we listen closely, we will find that many of them do not believe much differently than we do today. We may find that we can learn from them, that they may even inspire us to new, grand movements of the Spirit that can change the world forever.

In this book we celebrate those who were told they were no longer "part of the family," and welcome them back home. For heretics are not evil people who lived a long time ago. They are in fact our ancestors, people of sincere faith who followed their own convictions, even to the grave. Ancestors who ultimately only have to answer to one judge, and that judge is not us, but the God who calls them—and us—to genuine faith, however odd it may look to others.

Rock of Ages, your love and compassion for us remains steadfast and true even as our ideas, theologies, and orthodoxies have never stopped changing. Help us to cling to a strong and steady love such as yours, and to find within ourselves the generosity of heart to extend that kind of strong and unfailiing love to others, no matter their beliefs or struggles. For we ask this in the name of one who never called himself a Christian, even Jesus Christ. Amen.

⊕ *Adapted from a sermon preached at Grace North Church June 20, 1998.*

1 | The Jewish Christians

I n the first part of the twentieth century, a book was published that began a firestorm of criticism and controversy that has continued right up to the present day. The book was Albert Schweitzer's *The Historical Jesus*. In some ways this book cemented the parting of the ways for fundamentalists and progressives in Christian theology, often within the same denominations. More than that, though, it has fueled the imaginations of three generations of scholars attempting to lift the veil of legend and tradition to get at the "real Jesus" underneath.

This is a quest most of us appreciate. It is obvious that as Christianity has grown, developed, and spread throughout the world, people have added their own ideas to the mix until nearly every variety of those calling themselves "the elect" would have been completely unrecognizable to the first century peasant known as Jesus. Of course we want to see "behind the curtain" of time, we want to get at "the real deal," to figure out what this Jesus guy himself thought he was about, rather than what centuries of tradition have said he asserted.

The problem is that we have very little reliable evidence. The scriptures we have in the New Testament have been edited and re-edited by the victors of the church's early doctrinal disputes. Many of the writings of those who held unusual opinions about Jesus have been destroyed, or lost to the ravages of time. Secular evidence of Jesus' ministry is slim, consisting only of a very few passages in the writings of Flavius Josephus, a Jewish scholar hired by the Roman Empire to chronicle the history of the Jewish people.

So is it possible to discern Jesus' original mission, or his original teachings? Is it possible to know where things "went wrong" in Christianity? These were questions that haunted me recently as I was researching information about the early church. I believe I came to an affirmative answer to those questions in the course of my studies, but this also led me to a dilemma: if it was possible to uncover the historical Jesus, was it not then imperative that I also follow this man, and whatever teachings my research brought to light? And what if that meant leaving behind everything I had come to know as Christianity?

These were the questions and doubts that I have wrestled with for the last year, and which ultimately led me to write these sermons. Who was the historical Jesus? And what were the teachings of his earliest disciples?

We find the answers to these questions in part in our own Bibles, in the book of Acts. Now, as Acts records, there were two early Christian communities; the most important was the church at Jerusalem. This church was led by James the Just, who, Paul tells us, was the flesh-and-blood brother of Jesus. As Jesus' brother, James had a lot of power in the early Christian community. Disputes were brought to him to decide, especially in matters of doctrine. The Jerusalem community was made up entirely of Jews. They did not think of themselves as a separate religion at the time. They were simply Jews who believed that the messianic promise had been fulfilled in their own lifetime. They worshipped in the synagogues, and continued to celebrate the festivals and holy days of their native faith. They sent out missionaries to the Jewish communities in Syria, and met with much success.

Following the teachings of the Rabbi Jesus might have continued as a school within Judaism were it not for another visionary, Saul of Tarsus. At first a vicious persecutor of the new messianic sect, Saul had a mystical experience on the road to Damascus and thereafter became the self-appointed missionary to the gentiles. As Luke records in the book of Acts, Paul had great success in converting gentiles to this odd Jewish sect, and you would expect that the Christians at Jerusalem would be ecstatic about his success. The truth is, they were appalled. For one thing, Paul was teaching doctrines to the gentiles that differed substantially from what James was teaching in Jerusalem, especially as regards the importance of the Law.

For the Jerusalem Christians, a gentile could certainly convert, but would have to subject him or herself to Jewish purity laws, including circumcision. Paul taught that adherence to the Law was optional, and not necessary to be counted a Christian if one was not Jewish. This put the Jewish Christians into an uproar. Who was this Paul guy, admitting people to their religion in a willy-nilly fashion that they did not approve of? Who did he think he was?

It all came to a head in the year 49CE, when Paul met James at the Council of Jerusalem to consider the question. At that time, after much heated discussion, James would make a decision that would seal the fate of his community: he decided that gentile converts would not have to keep the whole of the law, but instead, only to "abstain from things polluted by idols, and from fornication, and from strangled things and blood." In other words, anything that would cause a Jew to not be able to sit at table and eat with a gentile believer in good conscience.

This decision guaranteed for Paul the one thing his churches needed to thrive: legitimacy; for only those churches in communion with the one, great church in Jerusalem could claim legitimacy. But it also sealed the doom of the Jewish Christians. For not thirty years after this momentous decision, Jerusalem was destroyed by the Romans, and the Jewish Christians fled into permanent exile and obscurity.

The Jewish Christians settled in southern Syria, very near Galilee, where Jesus spent so much of his ministry. They continued to meet in the synagogues and to follow the teachings of the Rabbi, which they believed had fulfilled the Law of Moses. They came to call themselves the "*ebyonim*" or the "Ebionites," which is Hebrew for "the poor," since they believed wealth was an evil to be avoided. They survived in this little pocket of the Middle East for nearly four hundred years, even as the Pauline churches grew up around them, hopelessly outnumbering them, and eventually even deriding them as heretics.

How could this happen? How could the original church, led by Jesus' own family for generations, come to be seen as heretical? On the surface of the biblical record we can see that the Pauline Christians might see them as heretics for insisting that the Law was still binding, at least upon themselves as Jewish Christians. But we must remember that the book of Acts is written by Luke, a gentile and a convert to Pauline Christianity, who wanted to downplay any doctrinal differences with the Jerusalem church.

To determine the real nature of the Jewish Christians' teachings we will have to go to those sources among their own writings which remain. Fortunately, a good many of the writings of the Ebionites survive in a collection attributed to St. Clement. These Pseudo-Clementine writings not only contain alternate versions of many of the events in Acts, but also preserve some of the sermons of Peter, which many scholars believe to be authentic.

What is so amazing about the Ebionite writings is what they reveal about the teachings of the early Jerusalem Christians, teachings which have either been whitewashed by the Pauline churches or expunged from memory altogether. More astounding yet is how closely those teachings square with the findings of the "historical Jesus" scholars.

How many folks today have a problem with the idea of the virgin birth? How many folks have difficulty with the doctrine of the substitutionary atonement? Even if you have no objections to these long-revered doctrines, it will come as no surprise to you that lots of people today do. And if you find you do have trouble with these doctrines, you may find that you have something in common with the Jewish Christians, with the Ebionites.

For these Christians, there was no virgin birth. Their church was headed up by Jesus' flesh-and-blood family. They knew better. Mary was James' mother, too, and he entertained no stories about her virginity. Perpetual maidenhood was a Greek ideal, not a Jewish one; the virgin birth was a doctrine which would simply have had no appeal for Jewish Christians.

But more important than this single doctrine was what it represented: a great parting of the ways in how Jewish Christians and Gentile Christians considered Jesus. While Gentile Christians leaned toward a high Christology, making Jesus the equal of God; Jewish Christians tended towards a low Christology, seeing Jesus as a great prophet, the equal or even the superior of Moses.

For Jewish Christians, Jesus did not die for anybody's sins. The idea of Jesus' death being a great sacrifice was a Pauline invention; Jews saw Jesus' death as the inevitable martyrdom in store for any-body who tried to buck the system. And in the estimation of the Jewish Christians, Jesus had bucked it big time.

The Jewish Christians believed that Jesus had come to complete the Law, a partial version of which had been given to Moses in the desert. They believed that Moses had received only a portion of the truth because the children of Israel were not yet mature enough to handle the whole of it. According to the Pseudo-Clementine writ-ings, God was very displeased with the practice of sacrifice and wanted it stopped altogether, for God is a compassionate deity who wishes nothing to suffer, not even animals. But Moses felt like this was too great a leap for the Israelites to make, and asked God for a compromise: to allow them to continue to sacrifice, but only to Yahweh and no other god.

God considered this an acceptable compromise, but promised that another prophet would come who would complete and fulfil the law, putting an end to temple sacrifices altogether, and causing the law to live in the hearts of men and women everywhere.

This may not be so far from how Jesus actually saw himself. The Gospels relate that Jesus said he had come "not to abolish the law, but to fulfill it," and that he prophesied more than once about the destruction of the temple. Jesus saw himself not as the founder of a new religion, but as a reformer of Judaism. The Jewish Christians saw him in the same way, and insisted that anyone who wished to follow Jesus must do so as a Jew.

As time went on, and the Jewish Christians took to calling them-selves Ebionites, they developed legalistic traditions of their own which were not reflective of their early Jerusalem forbears. In devel-oping their ideas about abolishing sacrifice, they went so far as to stop eating meat as well. They took their ideas of poverty to extremes, eschewing private property, and eventually living in impoverished communitarian ghettos on the margins of Syrian soci-ety. They began adding more and more prohibitions to the Law, striving for an escalating spiritual purity that must have seemed to them forever just out of reach. Finally, the community gave up the ghost in the fourth century, and what was left of the original

followers of Jesus were either re-absorbed into Judaism or converted to Pauline forms of Christianity.

What can we learn from these, the most original of Christians? It
is certainly quite a shock to discover that much of what modern
scholarship has to tell us about the historical Jesus was actually
affirmed and celebrated in the early Jerusalem church. It affirms for
us that those who hold a low Christology can just as legitimately call
themselves Christians as those who hold a high Christology. But the
greatest lesson comes from its interaction with the Pauline church.
For in refusing to adapt, to change, to flow with the times and cultures around it, it had no hope for survival. Like anything living,
theology must be allowed to grow. Jesus' teachings were a great
adaptation of theology to the times, but instead of following their
leader's example and forging ahead into new creative theologies, the
Jerusalem Christians codified and nailed shut the new covenant of
Jesus, making it as inflexible—and later even more inflexible—as its
mother faith. The unfortunate thing about this is that it left
Christianity only one creative stream to flow into: Paul's. Even
though Pauline Christianity certainly had the creativity to appeal to
a much greater audience, it is tragic to think of what might have
been, had the Ebionites not been so legalistic or xenophobic.

And so it was that the original defenders of the faith became
heretics, scattered to the four winds to disappear forever. Or did
they? Certainly many of the teachings and leanings of the Ebionites
survive in many denominations, although certainly not all together
in one place. The low Christology of the Jewish Christians can be
found in every one of the mainline denominations. Most of our sem-
inaries teach the historical Jesus as foundational, as the starting point
for all later theologies. James would have been pleased, I think.

The legalism of the later Ebionites is found today in many forms
of Evangelical Christianity. Baptists, Assemblies of God, and many
other fundamentalist sects teach—in practice if not in theory—a
very similar sort of adherence to the Law as was held by the
Ebionites. Those not in conformity are very quickly shunned and
outcast. Even the Ebionite penchant for vegetarianism survives in
tandem with your more standard-brand legalism in the Seventh-Day
Adventist denomination, which claims this early Christian community as a forerunner.

Also claiming the Jerusalem heritage are, oddly enough, the

Unitarian Universalists, who quite rightly remind us that the early Christians at Jerusalem had no concept of a trinity, and were, in fact, Unitarian Christians who saw God as one, and Jesus as simply a great teacher, much as Unitarian Universalists do today. The UU's also remind us that there was a great deal of diversity of opinion about Jesus in the first century and seek to provide a safe container for such diversity in their own churches in modern times.

It was after discovering the existence of the Ebionites that I was struck with my great crisis of faith several months ago. Now that I knew all this about Jesus and the early Church, I had become convinced that the only way to follow Jesus with any integrity was to become a Jew. I was terrified that God was calling me to refound the ancient heresy of Ebionitism in the present day! After all, it has a lot going for it: a believable Jesus, a strong moral code, and vegetarianism to boot!

But I finally realized that I am not, after all, a Jew. I am a Christian reared in a Pauline tradition, and as much as I revere Judaism, its traditions and its disciplines, I also had to admit that those traditions were not mine. I would have to make peace with the church I was given, with 2,000 years of creativity and growth and change. In the end I began an association with the Unitarian Universalists, and in this way I was able to claim the heritage of the Ebionites for my own, while at the same time affirming an open-ended approach to theology that could continue to grow and speak to the times.

So what are we to do with this information about the early Jewish Christians? I suggest that we stop ignoring them and begin some earnest study of their gospel and traditions, for we may yet have much to learn from them about the historical Jesus. I also suggest that we dispense with the term "heretic" with which Eusebius saddled them in the fourth century, and simply welcome them home into the family of believers of which they were the first and founding members.

Blessed are you, Sovereign of the Universe, for you sent us Jesus as your mouthpiece; who taught us that it is obedience and not sacrifice which is pleasing in your sight; and who taught us to view tradition both critically and creatively. Help us to welcome home into our embrace these brothers and sisters who followed you with their whole hearts, who sought to call their fellow Jews into a renewed covenant with you, and who called

Jesus not only friend, but family member and rabbi. For we ask this in the name of the one who went to his death for the purity of his faith, even Jesus Christ. Amen.

⊕ *Preached at Grace North Church July 5, 1998.*

2 | The Gnostics

After I left the fundamentalist church of my childhood, I made the questionable decision to attend a Southern Baptist college. My mother says "I told you so" now, but at the time it seemed like the thing to do, since my Grandmother had offered to pay my tuition, and I didn't feel I had many other options for an education. So off to California Baptist College in Riverside, California I went.

What I wasn't prepared for was all of the inner work that was waiting for me. Coming into this evangelical environment—as an outsider for the first time—I was able to notice a lot more than ever before, especially the subtle interior happenings that form the substance of our spiritual lives.

Much to my surprise, my inner process began to evidence itself in a most distressing fashion. I began writing poetry, that, quite frankly, scared the socks off of me. A character began to appear in my poetry that I can only describe as "The Monster God." To give you an example of these sorts of poems, I would like to read you one, titled "Unyummy":

God dropped in on Ungar Belfast just around lunchtime.
"AAARRR!!" God roared, and Pastor Henri Todd
was suddenly there to translate.

"He says 'The cold are yummy..."
"AAARRR..." Ungar shrunk in terror.
"...and the hot are extremely tasty with a bit of red wine."
"AAAARRRR!" God was enraged.
"...but the lukewarm, those he would spew out of his mouth!"
At this, God completely flattened Pastor Henri Todd
with the flat of his hand and ate him.
Then He spewed forth the Pastor,
who was whole again, if not a little shaken.
"Well," stammered the Pastor Henri Todd,
"In my case he would vomit perpetually."
God patted him on the head and smiled,
showing Ungar Belfast all his huge pointed teeth.

As you can imagine, I was terrified of what was flowing out of my pen. I was certain that God was going to send me to Hell for daring to think—let alone write—such thoughts. And then, of course, it struck me: the God who would send someone to Hell for being creative is precisely the sort of ridiculous character pictured in my poems. It certainly couldn't be anything like the *real* God, if there was such a thing. I decided that what was coming out of me was important for some reason I did not yet fathom, and decided that, damnation or no, I should go with it. And so "The Monster God" became a fixture in my poetry writing for many years to come.

I am not the first person to have this intuition that God is a monster, of course. Nor am I the first to write about it. As far back as the first century there were Christians who held a very similar opinion. They were called "Gnostics" and are probably the most famous, and most misunderstood, of all the ancient Christian heresies.

There were many varieties of Gnosticism in the ancient world, not all of them Christian. One teaching that the many varieties of Gnostics held in common was the belief in a radical dualistic split between matter and spirit. Deriving this part of their philosophy from Persian sources, Gnostics held that the flesh—and all things material—were evil, being the creation of a wicked demiurge, which Christian Gnostics identified with Yahweh, the god of the Hebrews.

In one Gnostic cosmology, Sophia (or Holy Wisdom) somehow "slipped out" of the Pleroma, where the Godhead resides. Hoping to regain her place through imitation, she gave birth to a demiurge,

Yahweh, and instructed him to create a world. This Yahweh did, but then, having gained a taste of divine power, Yahweh rebelled against Sophia and contrived to keep Adam and Eve enslaved forever.

The earth, then, for the Gnostics, was a prison-planet ruled by an evil tyrant. The soul would continue to reincarnate in this insufferable vale of tears until the power of Yahweh and his evil angels—the "archons"—could be broken.

Fortunately that is not the end of the story. During all of this the "true" God, observing these events from the Pleroma, decided to help humankind, who, though helplessly trapped in matter, nonetheless contain a spark of divinity which longs to rejoin the Godhead, if only it could escape the body and the earth. Thus, the highest God sent Christ in the form of a serpent to the garden to help Adam and Eve in their plight. Acting on the serpent's wise counsel, the pair ate of the fruit of the knowledge of good and evil, and their eyes were opened to their incarceration. But before they could eat of the other tree which would break the archons' power completely, Yahweh interceded and succeeded in keeping them captive, though no longer ignorant of their plight.

Over the next many centuries, people forgot the salvific message of the serpent, and turned him into the "bad guy" in the Genesis story. So in the fullness of time, the true God from the top of the Pleromic hierarchy sent the Christ to earth again—this time in the form of a man—to teach humanity how to break the power of the archons once and for all, and to woo Sophia back into the Pleroma. Christ, in the Gnostics' view, was not God, but was not human, either. Being a divine, angelic being, the Christ could not contaminate himself by actual contact with matter. This obscenity was avoided by merely seeming to be human. Far enough down the divine totem pole to live as a spiritual being amongst creatures of flesh, Christ nonetheless had no corporeal nature of his own, but took on the appearance of flesh in order to teach against the archons and thereby to liberate humanity.

A seeker who heard the Gnostic myth and desired to escape Yahweh and the evil archons underwent a variety of rituals designed to ready a person to receive *gnosis*, a Greek word meaning "knowledge." When *gnosis* came upon someone, it was generally an ecstatic experience, a type of enlightenment that freed one from the power of the archons so that upon one's death, one would be able to leave this planet, escape the wheel of transmigration, and rejoin the fullness of the pleroma.

This story really turns everything on its ear, doesn't it? But it is understandable in light of the cultural context it arose in. Those who were attracted to this teaching were people whose experience of this life was one of tragedy. We struggle with similar questions ourselves: "If God is all good, why is there evil in the world?" The Gnostics' answer to this question was that it is because God himself is evil, and his creation, corrupt and filled with death.

Gnostics dealt with this knowledge in diverse ways. Some felt that because the world is evil, one should withdraw from it and practice extreme asceticism. Others, however, went in entirely the other direction, figuring that since the flesh was corrupt anyway, it wouldn't hurt to enjoy it a little bit. Gnostic rituals were often orgiastic, or just plain odd. In one sect, the bread and wine of the Eucharist were consecrated by releasing snakes onto the altar. Anything which the snakes touched as they slithered around was considered consecrated.

Some taught that the only way to break the power of the archons was to engage in a ritual known as "The Bridal Chamber," which was very much like Tantra, in that the male ritually assumes the person of Christ, and the female participant ritually assumes the person of Sophia. Then they would have intercourse in this ritual setting, which would symbolize the healing of dualism, and effect their liberation from the power of the archons. One sect believed that there were 365 archons surrounding the planet, and you could only break their power one at a time. Therefore a believer had to enact "The Bridal Chamber" ritual 365 days in a row—without missing any days—and each time with a different partner. That's what I call spiritual discipline! The lengths some people go to for salvation...

Understandably, for the Orthodox church fathers, this kind of teaching was clearly unacceptable. In addition to being immoral, Gnostic teaching did violence to the very important Jewish teaching that the earth and God were very good indeed. They also felt that in denying that Jesus was a creature of flesh and blood, they missed the entire point of the incarnation. But "spirit beings" and angels are a whole lot more fun than regular people, so the church struggled with how to combat Gnostic teachings.

Finally, St. Ireneaus hit upon an idea that seemed to do the job.

In order to reinforce the teaching that Jesus had indeed come in the flesh, he began to speak of the bread and wine as becoming his literal body and blood. If, in the Eucharist, Christians could see the Holy Spirit descending upon matter and entering it, making it divine on a daily basis, before their very eyes, it would reinforce the notion that the Holy Spirit had done the same for Jesus. Seeing these material objects of bread and wine filled with holiness, it was not so great a leap to think that Jesus, a human being of real flesh and blood, could also be divine.

It was a brave doctrine to preach, and probably would not have been acceptable to the apostles, but then of course it was fifty years later, and the needs were different at that time. The idea of "transubstantiation" as taught by these early Gnostic-fighters is still with us, of course, for good or ill.

Ireneaus and the bishops who followed him were largely successful in keeping these Gnostic ideas from influencing the church, but not for long. For three centuries later a young man embraced a form of Gnosticism called Manicheeism which was very popular at the time, and spent eleven years as an ascetic trying to rid himself of the evils of the flesh. Unfortunately for us, he eventually he gave up and became the most influential Christian theologian the church has ever known, St. Augustine. Far from leaving his Manicheeism behind, he simply baptized it, and brought much of its world-hating theology into the church, lock, stock, and barrel.

From Augustine the church got its notions of sex being sinful, of women as evil beings bent on the destruction of unsuspecting and morally weak men, and of the earth as a corrupt and vile place. It is also Augustine who formulated for us the doctrine of original sin, the idea that we come into this world bad and only get worse as we go along.

There is a sense in which the early Gnostic-fighters failed utterly, for the very doctrines which they fought so hard to keep out of the Christian church were, with the advent of Augustine, enshrined as dogma. The continued refusal of the Roman Catholic church to ordain women or sexually active men is certainly a Gnostic holdover. Probably the most blatantly Gnostic churches today are the various evangelical sects, such as the one I grew up in, or such as those you see represented on almost any televangelism program. These sects perpetuate the ideas of the world being corrupt and the flesh as evil.

The vitriolic way in which they speak of sex is a dead giveaway. They also teach a very Gnostic form of salvation, promising that if you will go through their little ritual—pray a certain prayer—then you will be filled with the Holy Spirit and be free from the corruption of the world. In charismatic sects, this ritual is often attended by speaking in tongues or other phenomena which tends to equate salvation with an ecstatic experience. Shocking as it may seem to us, Gnostic teachings are much more prevalent in our churches today than are the early Christian notions of gender equality, or of the blessedness of Creation. What we have to learn from the Gnostics is very important: we have become them. Perhaps it is time to start fighting these ideas again.

To be fair, the point should be made that there were many valuable things which the Gnostics offered the world. In a time when most worship was ritualized and stale, Gnosticism held out a transformative *experience* of the divine that was hard to argue with. It also envisioned women as having a place in divinity, even if it was Sophia's fault that we are all in this mess in the first place. In early Gnosticism, it's still the woman's fault, even if she is divine. Jung wrote a good deal about how the Gnostics' cosmology is a model for psychological individuation, and when viewed from this perspective, Gnostic mythology can be very powerful and useful indeed.

I personally have found that this myth speaks to me very deeply as I continue to deal with "The Monster God" of my youth and in my poetry. I believe it may have much to offer to others of my generation, as well. For, like the Gnostics, we feel that we have been lied to about God. The image of God we have been given is of a harsh, even cruel, taskmaster who delights in torturing souls for eternity. We have also been told lies about this world being corrupt, about our very selves being corrupt.

And yet despite this, we know in our heart of hearts that this earth is a blessed place, that we are holy and valuable beings. We have been called the most cynical generation there ever was, and I agree with that assessment. We have been lied to, and we won't be taken in again. I believe this is why there are so few Generation Xers in church. We don't trust you. And with good reason.

This is precisely why the Gnostic myth can be instructive to us. If young people follow the myth they will see that the God they were given as children is indeed a monster, but is also a pretender to the throne. He is not the real God. There is, in fact, another God beyond him, behind him. A true and good God who calls us to health and wholeness; to right relationship with ourselves, with each other, and with the earth.

This is the spiritual journey of young people today, I believe. It has certainly been my journey. The monster God is very much a reality for me and for anyone who has been wounded by an abusive image of God. And for us, salvation does come through knowledge. For we are freed from the power of this demiurge once we bite of the fruit, see that he is a false God, and choose to enter into relationship with the true God who is beyond all dualities, who calls us friends and lovers, who made this earth and called it "Good."

Creator God, you made us for communion with you, and yet in our struggle to understand evil, we have ourselves perpetuated much of it. Help us, as followers of Jesus, to reject those images of you which are false, and to embrace the goodness at the heart of Creation which we know in our deepest souls includes the earth and ourselves. Give us discernment and true sight, that we might keep those things in our tradition that are useful, and discard those which are not, that we may pass on to the next generation a more true and healing vision for the sake of your church and this entire blessed community we call "earth." For we ask this in the name of one who did not despise the flesh, and wishes us to love it more, even Jesus Christ. Amen.

⊕ *Preached at Grace North Church July 19, 1998.*

3 | Montanism

When I was in junior college, I began making my first bold forays into churches which were other than the Southern Baptist variety that I grew up in. One church in my home town of Benicia had broken from the Southern Baptist fold and embraced a "contemporary" style of worship which included dancing in the aisles and the occasional eruption into ecstatic utterance, which we called "speaking in tongues." Now, I had been going to this church for about a month, mostly because of a cute girl named Jesse who was a member there, and although nobody had started speaking in tongues yet as far as I had seen, I had heard of it happening. I enjoyed the bouyant worship style and the hypnotic choruses, and I even felt a little closer to God when I raised my hands in worship along with everybody else. It was difficult to admit to my family at the time, especially my grandmother, that I was going to a non-Southern Baptist church. And like the dutiful guardian of my spiritual life that she was, Grandma invited herself along one Sunday night for prayer meeting. She had to "check out" this new group her grandson had fallen in with. Things were going well for the first half hour of the service. The praise music was lovely, and even my grandmother was singing along.

Then it happened. Disaster struck. One woman near the front stood up and started jabbering incoherently in something that

sounded like some kind of pidgin Hebrew. I froze in my seat, too terrified to look at my grandmother. Before I knew what was happening, another person on the other side of the room stood up and
announced that he had received an interpretation from the Holy
Spirit. According to St. Paul, the Corinthian Christians should not
speak in tongues unless there was an interpreter present. Our interpreter proceeded to pour forth a jumble of affirmations and warn-
ings in a mixture of bad King James English and modern slang.
Surely the Holy Spirit who inspired the King James translators had
not lost his touch, I thought! I was mortified by what was obvious-
ly some kind of sham performance by those in the crowd, and
embarrassed by what my stolid-and-staid Baptist grandmother was
going to think. When I finally got up the nerve to glance over to her,
I could swear I saw her listing to one side, about to fall over, but it
could have been my imagination. Driving home after the service, she
said only one thing to me: "Well, at least it was handled scriptural-
ly." Meaning at least there had been an interpreter, regardless of how
suspect the interpretation.

This experience with my grandmother left me aware that youth-
ful exuberance in worship, and the scorn of those more set in their
worship ways, is nothing new in Christian history. We see the evidence of this kind of dissension as far back as the second century,
when, in the year 156 CE, a young man named Montanus was bap-
tised and came up out of the water speaking in tongues and
announcing the revival of the primitive Christian church. Montanus
was from Phrygia in Asia Minor, the same place where the wild
Bacchic cults had their center, and coincidentaly enough, the very
same place that gave birth to the charismatic Islamic sect, the Sufis.
Who knows just what it was that caused such similar ecstatic movements across ten centuries and three religions—maybe it was something in the water!

In any case, Montanus believed that the church had become hierarchical and deadening to the spirit. Instead, he taught that God
inspired everyone in the church to a variety of ministries, much as
Paul had done. He said that every Chrsitian could be inspired, and
that the whole church could become "like a lyre, with the Spirit
playing upon her." He called all who would follow the true Gospel
of Christ to proclaim this "new prophecy." Montanist church services were often cacophonous affairs, with everyone being permitted to

sing, prophesy, dance, or speak in tongues at any time the Spirit moved them. Wonder what my Grandmother would have made of that!

Montanus also accused the churches leaders of being morally lax and demanded celebacy of his followers. He forbade second marriages and doubled the length of many of the proscribed fasts, even introducing a new kind of fasting called "zerophagy" or the eating of dry foods only. Montanus taught that after baptism the person was a new and sinless person in Christ, and must never sin again, because, according to Montanus, you just don't get any second chances. Montanus thus taught that penitents were not to be allowed back into the church.

He also taught that no Christian should serve in the military and inspired his followers to be a great party of martyrs. Many of them were, in fact, successful in this venture. Many of the preachers in the movement were women, two of whom served as Montanus' closest disciples and helpers. Montanus also taught the imminent return of Christ, that he would reign for a thousand years in the New Jerusalem, which was supposed to descend out of the sky right over Phrygia, conveniently enough.

Now, you might think that all of this wild carrying on in church and harsh criticism of her clergy might have brought the anger of the church's hierarchy down upon Montanus, but surprisingly, many bishops were moved by the Montanists' courage and spiritual fervor, and for twenty years the movement spread unhindered as far away as Gaul.

About 171, however, one bishop called Apollinarius had had enough, and he began to rebuke the Montanists, and forbade their teaching in his jurisdiction. Finally, in 177, at a council meeting which included both the bishop of Rome and St. Irenaeus, Montanism was declared a heresy.

It is odd that it was declared a heresy, because although many of their practices were unusual, and their worship chaotic, they did not actually teach anything heretical. The apostles had taught the imminent return of Christ, after all, and the length of fasts and such things were matters of tradition, not dogma. No, what really got the Pope's goat was the Montanists' disdain for the heirarchy of the church. It was also felt that Montanism was dangerous because of its over emphasis on the second Advent (which hindered long-range planning), its tendency to whip worshippers into a neurotic frenzy, and its demands for celibacy from everybody, which would have stopped the growth of the church right there! Thus, just as the movement was starting to really take off across the West, Rome dropped the ax.

Of course, this just added fuel to the fire. Many Christians who were not enamoured of the church's administration found like minds in the movement, and it even attracted such notable thinkers as Tertullian, who was the first Christian writer to dare to posit that the Holy Spirit was God to an equal degree as the Father and the Son. Tertullian was appalled that the institutional church was leaving behind Jesus' humanity, emphasizing his divinity so much that he was in danger of becoming simply a distant mythological figure. In the Montanists, however, Tertullian found others who embraced Jesus' humanity, even while denying much of their own. Though Tertullian and others added intellectual weight and a certain amount of prestige to the movement, it languished after being declared heretical, and only survived in pockets for a little while longer.

Despite the fact that Montanus himself was declared a heretic, and the movement he inspired condemned, many of the things he taught have remained alive and active in the church's history. The tendency to proclaim Christ's immediate return has cropped up here and there for the last two thousand years, reaching a fevered pitch most recently in the 1970s with the publication of Hal Lindsey's *The Late Great Planet Earth* and other God-shock bestsellers. The same time period saw the charismatic renewal movement spread from the margins of evangelical Christianity to nearly every denomination in the world, including the Roman Catholic Church. In almost any large city in the U.S. it is now possible to find a "Charismatic Mass" in a Catholic or Episcopal church. The fastest-growing liturgical church in the United States, in fact, is an Old Catholic offshoot called the Charismatic Episcopal Church, whose bishops were consecrated by the very same bishop who ordained me eight years ago.

The most visible charismatics are still evangelicals, however, and like the early Montanist movement, many of their most celebrated preachers have been women. Aimee McPherson, the mother of the modern charismatic movement began her preaching ministry in the early part of this century, and even though many charismatic denominations refuse to ordain women, there is no doubt that those same churches would not even be in existance today were it not for the preaching of this fiery woman who had mastered the art of showmanship.

What do we have to learn from these charismatic Christians? Quite a bit, I believe. From them we see that the Holy Spirit will not be kept in a box defined by our own culture or sense of propriety. Instead, God is a soaring bird, who lights where it will upon the head of anyone God chooses to carry the Gospel message. They also show us that worship does not have to be strictly ordered or nap-inducingly sober to be genuine. I dare any of you to try to convince a Black Baptist Church to hang up their tamborines and start using the 1928 *Book of Comman Prayer.* It ain't gonna happen, folks! Stomping feet and raised hands are just as pleasing to God as the Collect for Purity. And darn it all, sometimes when the spirit moves, I've got to move a little, too; and there ain't nothin' wrong with that.

But St. Ireneaus wasn't completely out to lunch, either. There are indeed reasons to be cautious about Charismatic worship, for it is in the context of such high emotionalism that reason and compassion can get lost. My wife Kate was brought up in what is now the largest of the Charismatic denominations, the Assemblies of God. In her church, she remembers that a famous evangelist held a month-long revival. There were services every night of the week, and each one of them raised the emotional ferver of the night before up another notch, until by the end of the month the church was nearly bank-rupt, scores of people had left the fellowship of the church feeling manipulated and abused, and a church split almost tore the com-munity apart. Yes, Kate's church had indeed been taken for a wild ride, but one has to doubt whether the Holy Spirit was really in the driver's seat.

Like Ireneaus we should remember that none of the things Montanus was condemned for were worthy of condemnation in their own right. Montanus taught no heretical doctrines, as such. But he did take things to the edge, and although God often meets us in such wild places, God rarely drives us there.

Life-giving and prophetic God, you do not call us to a dead and love-less worship, but to the true quickening of our souls. You desire the earnest praise of our lips, and even the ecstatic dancing of our feet. Inspire us, even as you inspired Montanus, to explore a lively relationship with you, to claim the gifts of ministry which your Holy Spirit affords to all who will follow you, and grace us with a good dose of Anglican reason to balance prophesy with common sense, so that this may be a place of true communion for the praise of your holy name and for the cure of souls, for we ask this in the name of our true healer, even Jesus Christ. Amen.

⊕ *Preached at Grace North Church August 20, 1998.*

4 | Monarchianism

The late seventies were a surreal time for most of us, but particularly for me as a teenager. I was at the time a raging fundamentalist, and at the age of 16, a licensed minister of the Gospel. A 16-year-old with a license to preach can be a dangerous thing indeed, and in fact I'm surprised I emerged from this period of my life without getting roughed up or worse! It was my habit, every Thursday night, to DJ at a local roller rink. I would play disco with Christian lyrics, and halfway through the evening, I would shut down the rink, ask everybody to clear the floor, grab my 90-pound red Bible and stand up on one of the tables to preach to the hapless skaters.

Now, admittedly, Thursday was billed as "Christian night" so I didn't exactly get in trouble for these shinanigans, but there were more than a few "Christians" present who didn't appreciate the program. To be honest, I would count myself one of those, now!

Some of the most vocal dissenters from this program, however, were a visiting group of Pentacostals who were known to us as "Jesus Only" Pentacostals. I honestly don't know the exact name of their church or denomination, but I was intrigued by their theology, which they explained in the context of critiquing mine. It seems that the Jesus Only folks were not trinitarians, but in their own way, Unitarians. They believed that there was no God the Father or Holy

Spirit—there was only Jesus. Jesus created the world, Jesus died on the Cross, and Jesus fills us with his spirit and causes us to speak in tongues.

"What a curious theology!" I thought at the time, and promptly responded that they were full of hooey. Fortunately, I have grown a lot since that time and have discovered increasingly more sophisticated methods for describing someone's theology as "hooey," even if perhaps they are not so colorful.

I have also come to discover that the Jesus Only folks are not so unique as I thought. They are, in fact, a version of a very old teaching known as Monarchianism.

As we have discussed in earlier sermons in this series, in Christianity's infancy there was no clear-cut description of exactly who Jesus was. We had the titles attributed to him by Paul, and Paul certainly referred to him in terms approaching divinity, but Paul also at times speaks of Jesus as a creature, a being created by God.

Unfortunately, Jesus wasn't around anymore to drill about such specifics, and apparently no one had thought to ask him about this stuff when he was, and so great variety of teachings arose in the church. As we have seen, the Jewish Christians simply felt he was a great man, a prophet who was chosen by God and "adopted" as his Son. Then there were those who went the complete other direction, saying like the Jesus Only folks that Jesus was fully and completely—and the only—God. And of course, there were people postulating every conceivable position in between as well.

Monarchianism first began to emerge as a distinct teaching around the beginning of the third century. Basically, the name comes from the word "Monarch" and refers to the fact that God alone is King, God alone is God, in reaction to much of the trinitarian thought that was also beginning to gain a foothold amongst the bishops of the time. Whereas Trinitarianism kind of "spread the divinity around" amongst three distinct persons, Monarchianism fiercely affirmed the unity of God, and relegated the other persons of the trinity to either subordinate positions, or as facets or "faces" of the one God and King.

Monarchianism was usually expressed in one of two forms, dynamic and modalistic. Now the dynamic form is close to the position claimed by the Ebionites, or the Jewish Christians. These Monarchians taught that Jesus was an ordinary man in whom the power, or *dynamis* of God was pleased to dwell. Thus Jesus was not God, but God's power was *in* Jesus. In this scheme, the Holy Spirit, too, is subordinate to the Father, who sends it where "he" will, much as he sent his *dynamis* into Jesus. This variety of Monarchianism gradually evolved into one of the greatest heresies of all time, Arianism, but that is the subject of another sermon.

The more popular form of Monarchianism, however, was "modalistic." Modalistic Monarchianism, while difficult to say ten times in swift succession, is a very attractive teaching indeed, and you might be suprized to find that there are a great many Christians worshipping in our churches today who would not find a whole lot in this teaching to disagree with. Modalistic Monarchianism says that there is only one God, but that God has three "faces" or modes of interacting with human beings. One mode is as Creator or father of all; but God also reveals himself as Redeemer, through the persona of Jesus; finally God has also revealed himself to the church through the ministry of the Holy Spirit, our comforter and encourager. Modalistic Monarchians believed that history was divided into three periods: the era of the Creator was past, as was the era of the Redeemer, for Jesus had come and gone. They believed they were in the era of the Spirit, and when the mission of the Spirit is finished, as David Christie-Murray says, "God will put away his three actor's masks for good and resume the single, simple, undifferentiated being that he fundamentally is."

Sounds very reasonable, doesn't it? My question is, why stop with three? Aren't Vishnu and Buddha and Ahura Mazda "modes" of God's self-revelation? The beauty of Modal Monarchianism is that it allows a great deal of inclusivity when one thinks about other religions and considers through which faces God has dealt with human beings—in all times and in all places. I might consider myself to be a modalist in just this way. I leave you to consider this possibility for yourself.

Modalist Monarchians have sometimes been referred to by another name, equally hard to pronounce, called "Patripassianists" which means, "the father suffers." This refers to the Crucifixion, where, since Jesus is just a mode of God the Father, in truth it is God the Father who suffered on the cross. Patripassianists, then, teach that God the Father took upon himself human flesh, and becoming the Son, was crucified and died. And through his almighty power, he raised himself from the dead.

This is not very much different from the Jesus Only folks I encountered as a teenager, who seem to simply have replaced God the Father with Jesus. The modalism is nearly identical, if unusual.

Monarchianism was declared a heresy within a hundred years of its emergence, and there are few charismatic individuals to which one can tie the teaching. It was more of an amorphous exploration as the fledgling Christian church struggled within itself to understand how to embrace one God who had revealed Godself in so many diverse ways. Monarchianism was simply the conservative pole of the argument, asserting absolutely the unity of God, and often condemning other Christians as being idolators and polytheists.

Even though the movement was eventually put down or absorbed by the majority of orthodox thinkers, we shouldn't consider that the argument has been definitively settled. In fact, there is still quite a bit of dissension about this very issue amongst Christian churches today, dissension that, in fact, was instrumental in the great schism between Orthodoxy and Catholic Christianity.

The original text of the Nicene Creed reads: "I believe in the Holy Spirit, who proceeds from the Father" and ends the clause there. In the West, however, for the last 1,000 years we have accepted an amendment to that august document, that was never ratified by any council of the entire church. We add what is called the "*filioque*" clause, which means "and the Son." Thus, in the West, we say, "I believe in the Holy Spirit, who proceeds from the Father *and* the Son."

Since Rome made this change without the consensus of the whole church, you can imagine that it caused quite a ruckus, because it quite literally set the theology of God on its ear.

In the East, the hierarchy of power firmly favors the Father. The point of the triangle is at the top, where the Father is, and the Son and Spirit are subordinate under him. But in the West, we've turned this triangle on its side, so that the Son and Father are of equal authority, with only the Spirit being subordinate. The Monarchianists would, of course, favor the older formulation, even though they would reject much of the content of the Nicene Creed, which uses language that, quite deliberately, excludes Monarchian teachings.

So what are we to make of the Monarchianists? Are they evil

heretics that should be shunned from Christ's fellowship? Hardly. They merely represent one of the many options open to Christianity in the early centuries of its expansion in understanding Jesus' relationship to God. And, I must say, it is a much more palatable and intuitive formula than the trinitarian one we have been stuck with, in my humble opinion. They were labeled heretics after only a century of development. There have even been Monarchianist popes, amazingly enough, and whether they are familiar with the term or not, many Christians today actually envision God in a way more similar to Modal Monarchianism than to orthodox trinitarianism.

So why were they finally defeated? Because Christians, like most people, find ambiguity difficult to tolerate. In the first few centuries of the church, when all the "heresy hunting" was at its most fevered pitch, Christians were anxious to nail down a definitive theology. Most of the common people cared little what it would turn out to be, but the Bishops argued long and hard, for very often there were rival bishops in the opposing camps. Whether or not a bishop got to keep his see frequently depended on whether one's theological party won the debate or not.

We in the twentieth century are no less anxious when it comes to ambiguity, but because of the findings of quantum mechanics and other "fuzzy logic" sciences, we are at least aware that certainty is an illusion, an ever-receding goal that we can never reach. "Not knowing" is part of what makes us human, and standing strong and brave in a place of "not knowing" is a sign of spiritual maturity. I am always grateful to meet a person who is comfortable saying "I don't know" and always wary of someone who says they do.

I'd like to close this sermon by honoring someone who lived out his ambiguity with relish. When I first met Ed Vanek, I wasn't sure what to make of him. He was kind of an odd little man with a quick tongue and an infectiously kind demeanor. He lived out his ambiguity in a way that was for me, at first, unsettling. For one thing, he seemed to think it was no great deal to be an active member of more than one congregation; and I must say, he was active. This taught me a great deal, to the extent that I now hold memberships in three very different Christian denominations, while working for a fourth.

The most challenging obstacle I had to overcome with Ed, however, involved communion. Every week, while administering the bread, I was very aware that Ed would take the bread from my hand,

and without even seeming to disguise his actions, put the piece of commuion bread in the pocket of his jacket. Now when I first came here, I was much more of a Catholic priest than I am today, and I was horrified by this behavior. I mean, what was he doing with that bread? Did his collection of bits of the "body of Christ" build up week after week in his pocket? Did he add every week's bit of communion bread to a ball of old bread when he got home? Did it get thrown away by the dry cleaners, or did he perhaps feed it to the birds later on?

Only God and Ed may ever know the answer to that question; but as I got to know Ed better, as I understood his quirky and endearing nature, and as I became less and less "fundamentalist" about my Catholicism, it began to matter less and less. What really mattered, I eventually realized, is that whether the bread ever made it to his mouth or not Ed came here because he felt fed by God in this place. Communion is simply an enacted metaphor for everything that happens within these walls. Ed may have put the bread in his pocket, but his communion with us was as real as any other. Ed may have put Jesus in his pocket, but I will carry Ed in my heart for a long, long time to come.

O God, who is our sovereign as well as our friend, help us to look with love upon those who view you with different eyes. For you come with power to those who need your power, and you come with healing in your wings for those who are infirm. Light upon us now with your Holy Spirit, and however we may understand you, move our hearts closer to yours, so that we may bid you with all sincerity, to "Come, and rule in our hearts forever." For we ask this in the name of the one who deigned to call you Father, even Jesus Christ. Amen.

⊕ *Preached at Grace North Church September 13, 1998.*

5 | Origen

I was in fourth grade when I caught my first whiff of constitution-al empowerment. We were living in Brownstown Township, Michigan, at the time, and the school district had started a bussing program similar to so many around the country. Consequently, I spent nearly an hour traveling both to and from school. Upset at this, as you might imagine, I complained to my parents. They suggested I write a letter to the president, who at that time was Richard Nixon. So, full of determination, I sat down and cranked out an angry letter to Nixon. Well, the president must have had his fill of angry letters from children that year, because I never received a reply, and consequently, I was never rescued from the evil bussing program.

What I did gain from this experience, however, was the knowl-edge that, although I may still have to fall into line behind the other sheep, I at least had the right to bleat. So it was that two years later, when I became irate that the "theory" of evolution was being taught in my school, I sat myself down again to dash off a letter of com-plaint to Jimmy Carter, who, after all, was a Southern Baptist just like me, and by all accounts should be just as upset about this as I was.

What surprised me, however, was that my father was not entire-ly behind my protest this time. He sat down at the dinner table with me and uttered a completely life-changing sentence. He said, "I don't think that the theory of evolution necessarily contradicts the Bible."

My head swam with suddenly unforeseen implications. I had always assumed that the Bible was meant to be taken literally. My father's utterance was my first inkling that there might be another way to approach the scriptural text. My father has since recanted his radical views, and now holds to a strict six-day creation scheme. But his momentary lapse into modern exegesis left me changed forever.

The fascinating thing about this is that Dad's explanation really wasn't all that modern. In fact it goes back all the way to the early third century when a Christian theologian named Origen wrote, "Who is so silly to think that God like some farmer actually planted a paradise eastwards of Eden?"

Instead of taking the biblical text literally, Origen read it symbolically. For him there wasn't a literal Garden of Eden, but the Garden was nonetheless a spiritual reality for each of us, a place of innocence that we have lost. He applied this "spiritual" approach in many voluminous commentaries on scripture, many of which still survive and still enjoy a healthy readership.

So who was this man, Origen, who seems so ahead of his time? And why are we considering him in our series on heresy?

The story starts in the late second century when a bishop in Alexandria named Demitrius established a school for pagans interested in studying Christianity. A man named Clement ran the school, and taught that pagan philosophy—especially Plato—had prepared humankind for the coming of Christ no less than the Old Testament had. In this school, Platonic philosophy was taken seriously by the Christian teachers. Platonism was their accepted worldview into which Christianity, after some pushing and prodding, fit very nicely.

This popular and successful school hit hard times, however, when Christians began being persecuted in Alexandria. Clement fled the country, and Demetrius went into hiding. Since no sensible person wanted to risk running the school, Demetrius appointed a young eighteen-year-old man by the name of Origen to the post.

Origen had been raised in a Christian home, and as a young man had been almost fanatical about martyrdom. His father had been martyred, and certainly Origen would have been, too, had his mother not hid his clothes so he couldn't leave the house. He never forgave her for that and continued to pine for martyrdom his whole life long.

Although they didn't have bussing, schools even then were integrated, gender-wise as well as racially. Origen was terrified at the prospect of teaching women, fearing that he may succumb to sexual passion. So taking Jesus' words "If thy hand offend thee, cut it off" in a more literal way than was his wont in approaching biblical texts, Origen made himself a eunuch for the glory of the Kingdom of God.

Origen was ascetic in other ways, as well. He was a vegetarian, subsisting largely on a diet of raw vegetables and beans, and he allowed himself only a few hours of sleep per night, so that he could have more time to study. He also refused payment for his teaching services, and sold his father's prized library of classical literature to support himself.

You might think it odd that a teacher would sell his books, but I have no doubt that Origen had everything in those books catalogued and available somewhere in his brain. For his life's work would be to understand the Christian mystery through the language, images, and ideas of Platonic philosophy.

By the year 210 CE, Origen had become a world-class celebrity, traveling throughout the empire giving lectures, sermons, and classes, as well as deciding doctrinal disputes. As you can imagine, this made him as many enemies as it did friends. Some folks accused him of being a new kind of Gnostic, but Origen saw himself as a defender of orthodoxy, and was not deterred.

Finally, Demetrius was moved to try to curb some of Origen's enthusiasm. The problem was that since Origen was just a teacher, Demetrius had very little control over him. He could fire him, but Origen's reputation would easily secure him another post. Best to "keep your friends close and your enemies closer." And Origen, not surprisingly, thought that all was as it should be: all theologians should be free to follow whatever line of inquiry occurs to them, he thought, without the censure of the church hierarchy. If something is of God, it will endure. If not, it will fade.

This scared Bishop Demetrius silly, and he perceived Origen as undermining the authority of the church. Origen thought that a simple solution could be reached. Demetrius should just ordain him, that way he could continue teaching, but he would be doing so with the authority of the church. Demetrius didn't like that idea at all, regarding such a move to be of the "out of the frying pan into the fire" variety.

The dilemma was finally resolved when Origen was lecturing in Caesarea. The local bishop there was a former student of Origen's, and when Origen asked him to ordain him, he did. Demetrius, of course, hit the roof and banished Origen, claiming that his priesthood was invalid because he was a eunuch! So Origen just moved to Caeserea, and settled in there, writing and teaching for another 20 years. During another wave of persecution, Origen was arrested and tortured on the rack, but his lifelong dream of martyrdom eluded him, and he eventually died of old age.

His teaching continued to garner fame long after his death, however, causing great rifts in the church. This went on for another two hundred years, at which time he was finally declared a heretic by the Fifth Ecumenical Council in the year 553.

"What were some of his ideas that were so threatening?" you might ask, and the answers may surprise you.

As I have said, Origen was a Platonist, and to understand his theology, we must begin here, with the Platonic concept of God as perfect, undifferentiated unity. As Robert Van de Weyer describes it, Origen taught that

> Originally God created angels that were "wholly pure," but at some moment these angels had become bored and rebellious, and so were cast out of heaven to live at a great distance. God then created the world to be a material home for these fallen angels, and as souls they now inhabit bodies. This is not a punishment, but rather an opportunity to learn afresh how to be united to God. The ultimate purpose of the soul, therefore, is to be restored to heaven by severing its material attachments, and ascending to God through prayer and contemplation.
> Robert Van de Weyer, *The Call to Heresy* (London: Lamp, 1989), p. 109.

For Origen the universe is very different than it is for most Christian theologians. The universe is good, for one thing, and the "fall" of humanity is not eternal or even necessarily evil. In his system human beings are reincarnated until they learn the lessons God has laid out for them to learn, and at the end of the ages, all beings, from the angels to Satan himself, will eventually learn of their error, and be reconciled to God.

What?? You might be saying. Reincarnation? Universalism? No eternal Hell? What's up with this guy? Was he completely out to lunch? No, just thoughtful, learned, optimistic, and hopelessly creative. Origen was considered a champion of orthodoxy in his day; it is hard for us to remember just how ill-defined orthodoxy was at that time. He was, of course, criticized later for being a Gnostic, and although there are many Gnostic elements to his teaching, it is a baseless and inaccurate accusation.

The only thing one might accuse Origen of is being too darned clever for his own good. There is no doubt that Origen had set out to become the most learned man in all of Christendom. His greatest work is the compilation of the *Hextapa*, a Bible that assembled all of the most ancient manuscripts available to him laid out in six parallel columns, sometimes stretching to as many as nine columns, when he could find fragments of even more ancient manuscripts.

As an author, he was unstoppable. Jerome once commented that Origen wrote more than anyone could possibly read. Epiphanius reports that his works number over 6,000 volumes. An astounding number, even if we remember that a "volume" could be quite short, the same way as there are 66 separate "volumes" in the Bible. It is reported that he employed seven full-time secretaries to transcribe his teaching, and even more scribes to copy and disseminate his writings.

And it is his writing—particularly his exegesis of scripture—that is his real claim to fame. For Origen was the first to suggest that the Bible needed to be read on two levels. The superficial, historical level, which was the normal way of understanding it; and the esoteric, spiritual level, which was his own innovation. Origen never denied the authority of scripture, he just decided he could pick and choose which level was authoritative. As David Edwards writes, "sometimes the literal meaning of a passage in the Old Testament seems to have so worried Origen that he hastened immediately to the spiritual meaning" (p. 67).

One example that will be immediately familiar to you is that of the Biblical book, "The Song of Solomon" or "The Song of Songs." Most of us are aware that the church has traditionally interpreted this erotic love poetry as being about the relationship between Christ and the Church. What most people are not aware of is that this is entirely Origen's idea, and is typical of his approach to scripture.

Origen was particularly fond of those writings attributed to Solomon, and considered Solomon's three books to be the cornerstone of Biblical teaching, and as providing the paradigm for spiritual growth.

Thus, Origen believed that spiritual growth had three stages: the first stage is virtue, which is addressed by the book of Proverbs. The second stage is detachment, which is elucidated by the book of Ecclesiastes. The third stage is contemplation, which can be read into the Song of Songs. Origen's formulation was understood in medieval times as the three-step process of Purgation, Illumination, and Union, but that is a corruption of his sometimes subtle ideas. A more profound understanding of his spiritual process was put forth by Meister Eckhardt, the great Rhineland mystic of the late middle ages, who named these stages the Via Positiva, the Via Negativa and the Via Creativa; and who added a fourth stage, the Via Transformativa, making the process of spiritual growth not linear, but cyclic (more on this in our chapter on Eckhart).

Eckhardt is not the only successor to Origen's ideas. Probably the most direct bequeathing of his mantle belongs to the great Swedish mystic of the eighteenth century, Emmanuel Swedenborg, whose own voluminous expositions of scripture use a method nearly identical to Origen's own. Although Swedenborg was not a proponent of reincarnation, his Christology and approach to scripture were very, very similar indeed. So close, in fact, that sometimes I wonder if Origen was not correct about the transmigration bit, and if Swedenborg was not, in fact, Origen reborn (more on Swedenborg later, too).

You will accuse me of veering into silly territory if I continue in this vein, so I'd like to close by affirming that for all of his unusual ideas, Origen was also without question the early church's greatest theologian. Even condemnation has not permanently sullied his reputation. And in this age when contemporary scholarship, as well as post-modern science, has called into question much of the superficial aspects of scripture, the time may be ripe for a deeper, more symbolic approach to return; an approach that shocked me as a child, and continues to intrigue me as an adult.

Creative and emotive God, you have given us keen minds and inquiring hearts to seek out that which is unknown to us. Help us to not be afraid when we embark into uncharted territory, but to trust in your Holy Spirit to speak the truth to us even when we do not know the way. Help us also to be open to the myriad levels of truth offered to us by your holy Word, which through not only history, but through myth, symbol, parable, and poetry speak to us of a love which cannot be grasped by mere words. Seize our hearts, O God, by your ungraspable Spirit, and move us to move ever closer to you. Amen.

⊕ *Preached at Grace North Church September 27, 1998.*

6 | Arius

Like most good little Southern Baptist boys, I was terrified of anything remotely heretical. Once I had begged for a bagel, and after my mother had purchased it for me, she informed me that it was a "Jewish donut." I was so terrified that God might strike me dead for partaking of such an interfaith morsel that I refused to eat it.

When I was a little bit older I went with my Catholic friend Mickey to see the hit comedy "Oh, God!" with George Burns and John Denver. Sitting by ourselves in the darkened movie theater, we actually stayed for most of two whole showings of the film, we both enjoyed it so much. But at one point in the film, I started to get nervous. John Denver was asking God a series of questions proposed by the world's religious leaders. One of them, which as an adult I might have seen coming, but which caught me completely off guard as a little boy, was "Is Jesus Christ your Son?"

The answer George Burns gives was frighteningly heretical. "Yes, Jesus was my son," Burns replied, but then he added, "Buddha was my son. And you, too, are my son." At these words, I froze in terror. Heresy! I felt like bolting out of the theater. In fact, I was afraid that if I didn't leave immediately, or in some other way make clear to God that I did not share these evil opinions, God would, again, strike me dead, or worse, damn my eternal soul to everlasting fire.

Fortunately, an unexpected grace occurred: somehow comedy won out over fear, and though trepidatious, and certainly looking around for signs of God's certain displeasure, I stayed for the close of the movie, and even stayed to watch most of it again.

What I didn't know at the time was that George Burn's heretical reply wouldn't always have been considered heretical. It echoes the teachings of an Alexandrian priest named Arius whose simple and humane theology butted heads with the teachings of more Platonic theologians in the fourth century of the church's history.

Unlike his opponents, Arius did not appeal to philosophy to support his arguments, but to the chagrin of his opponents, directly to scripture. He quoted it literally and liberally, and made quite a good case of it, so much so that even after his position had been decided against, Arian teachings continued to rock the Christian world for more than a century after his death.

In Arius' thinking, the salvation offered through Christ would have no meaning if he were some kind of divine being who was superior to human beings. He took quite literally the scripture which read "he was tempted in every way that we are," and asserted that Jesus must therefore have been capable of sin, even if he chose not to do it. If Jesus was possessed of some kind of supernatural willpower, Arius felt that his ministry could have no saving effect for us. It was because Jesus felt the same fear as we do, and struggled against the same kinds of temptation we do, and felt the same agony of uncertainty that we do that his death had any power. He remained faithful to God right to the very end, and therefore he is able to extend the grace of his perfect life to us.

Where Luke had written that "Jesus advanced in wisdom and in stature, and in favor with God and men," Arius interpreted it to mean that Jesus had completely free will, that he had made mistakes as a little boy, had to study hard to learn the Torah just like any other child. Eventually, he grew into perfection as he approached the age of accountability.

This perfect attending to the Spirit of God led Jesus to the Cross, which for Arius is the model for human living. Unlike his opponents, Arius taught that Jesus' struggle in the Garden of Gethsemene was real. Jesus was truly tempted to walk away from it all, to not go through with it. He wrestled with his conscience, and in the end, he remained faithful to God's calling and went to his death willingly. As

Robert van de Weyer writes, "The crucifixion is thus not the pre-ordained outcome of Christ's earthly life, which he had no choice but to accept; rather, it is the climax of Jesus' own spiritual pilgrimage."

For Arius, Jesus is the pattern which all who call themselves Christians should follow. And like Jesus, anyone who decides to walk in the way of the Cross may be equally considered "a son—or daughter—of God." This is supported by St. Paul, who wrote that we shall become "through faith God's sons in union with Christ Jesus." As Jesus was, so are we called to be.

Easier said than done. How did Jesus do it? What was in him that we do not possess that allowed him to overcome sin and provide a way of salvation? Arius' answer is, "Nothing that is not also in you and me"—namely, the Logos.

Now, the theology of the Logos goes back to Hillel, who sought to harmonize Judaic theology and Greek philosophy. Hillel drew a parallel between the figure of Holy Wisdom in the book of Proverbs and the Greek notion of the Logos, or the Word by which all things are defined and by whose agency the world had come into being. When John was writing his Gospel, he used the same parallel, implying that Holy Wisdom was the pre-incarnate Christ, who was also the same person as the divinity of the Greek philosophers, the Logos.

There were many varieties of Logos theology in the early Church, as you might expect. The Jewish Christians taught that the Logos descended upon Jesus at his baptism, whereupon he was "adopted" as God's Son. But for Arius, the Logos is that part of God that is common to all of humanity. The Logos is in everybody. What made Jesus' ministry effective is that he fully embraced the Logos within him, and thereby achieved perfect union with God. We, too, Arius taught, can completely embrace the Logos within us, and in fact, that is precisely the level of commitment that baptism calls us to.

Although his stressing of Jesus' humanity upset many of his rivals, it was his theology of the Logos that got him into real trouble. For while many bishops were already using Trinitarian language, making the Spirit and the Son equal to the Father, Arius was very clear that the Logos was subordinate to the Father. Arius even had doubts about the divinity of the Logos, asserting that the Logos was a power which issued forth from the Father, and was therefore a creature and not the Creator.

Again, Arius had strong scriptural support, quoting Paul's description of Jesus as "the first-born of all creation." For Arius, then, it was clear that there was a time when the Son was not, even if that time was a time before there even was time as we know it. (I hope you are still with me.) Arius once wrote, "The Son had a beginning but God is without beginning," which implies, of course, that the Son is not fully God.

Now if Arius had simply been content to be a parish priest and proclaimed his teachings only to his parishioners, we would not be talking about him now. Instead, he railed publicly against the heresy of his own bishop, Alexander of Alexandria, whom he accused of Modal Monarchianism, which we discussed in a previous sermon.

Alexander responded to Arius' challenge by calling a meeting of nearly a hundred bishops who did their "proper duty" and excommunicated Arius. But Arius was not lying down for any of this and had gained the support of bishops in Palestine and the Near East. This of course set up an impossible situation with accusations and mutual denouncements rocketing all over the early Church, threatening its peace and also its unity.

Finally, the Emperor Constantine intervened. He had embraced Christianity hoping it would unite his fragile Empire, and now the bishops whom he had elevated from the status of criminals to great positions of power threatened the very peace he had staked so much on. He wrote to both factions, ordering them to settle their differences over what seemed to him a trivial matter. His letter fell on deaf ears, unfortunately, and he finally called the Nicene Council to settle the dispute and, hopefully, return the empire to some semblance of order.

About three hundred bishops attended the Council, and Constantine himself presided, and even suggested some compromises (although he was no theologian himself, and was not even baptized until just before his death). The opposition, led by Alexander and one of his priests named Athanasius, was fierce, and quickly swayed the Council, so much so that when Arius rose to defend his position, many of the bishops put their fingers in their ears so as not to be stained by his heresy.

Much of the debate revolved around exactly what words to use to describe the Logos' relationship with the Father. Athanasius wanted to use *"homoousion"* which means "of the same substance." This implied that the Father and the Son were made of the same material, just as you might describe two coins made from the same metal. Other bishops suggested a compromise, wanting to use the word *"homoiusion"* which means "of similar substance." Ultimately, this made nobody happy, and as one ancient commentator put it, "the Church was convulsed by a diphthong."

The debate extended beyond the Council chambers, too, with the laity arguing the same positions in the streets. As David Christie Murray writes, "Gregory of Nyssa…described the money-changer who, when asked the exchange rate, replied with a dissertation on the engendered and non-engendered; the baker who informed his customer that the Father was greater than the Son; and the bath-attendant who told the would-be bather that the Son came from nothingness" (p. 46).

Athanasius won the battle, if not immediately the war, when all but two bishops affixed their names to his creed, and Arius and the two dissenting bishops were driven into exile. These days if you disagree with someone, you can go across the street to a different church, but they were playing for keeps in those days. Unfortunately for Athanasius, most of the bishops who signed his creed went back to their diocese and continued teaching just as they had before the Council, until popular and ecclesial support once more swung to Arius' favor, and this time it was Athanasius who was driven into exile.

It took half a century more of infighting and fierce theologizing before Athanasius' position was finally accepted by the whole of the church, and by then, both Arius and Athanasius had had their excommunications rescinded and died peacefully within the arms of mother church.

The creed decided upon at Nicea is familiar to us all. Although we use the simpler and earlier Apostles Creed in our worship at Grace North Church, most liturgical churches recite the verbose and complicated Nicene formula every week. I believe this is unfortunate, since the creed was created as an instruction against heresy and was never intended for liturgical recitation. It was incorporated into the liturgy for "blatant schismatic reasons," to justify the monophysite patriarch of Antioch in 473 (more on the monophysites in chapter nine).

Episcopal priest Richard Fabian (co-rector at St. Gregory Nyssan in San Francisco) advises ordinands that "if they must use the Nicene Creed in their parishes, they might march about waving American and Episcopal Church flags, while their church wardens tear up photographs of the Mormon Tabernacle: these gestures would express the custom's fundamental spirit..." (p. 29).

So is the Son eternal, or was there a time when the begotten was "not yet begotten"? Was Jesus a human being, tried and tempted just as you and I are, or was he some kind of superbeing who was above all of that? Although the church did come to some consensus by the fifth century, the debate has never really died down. There are many Christians today, in various denominations, who would feel more comfortable with Arius' theology than Athanasius', myself among them.

"Yes, Jesus was my son," George Burns' God said in the movie, "Buddha was my son, and you are my son." Heresy? I suppose it depends upon who you ask. If Arius had prevailed at the Council of Nicea seventeen hundred years ago, I reckon I would not have gotten such a knot in my tummy when I was a little boy.

Jesus, begotten of God, and deliverer of our souls, forgive us, for in our efforts to understand the mystery that is you we have often worked violence upon our brothers and sisters. Help us to be still before this mystery, to refrain from judging lest we ourselves know the pain of judgement, and give us grace to extend to those whose understanding is different from our own. For you are God for us, and you are the human one, and in this paradox we seek to rest eternally. Amen.

⊕ *Preached at Grace North Church September 27, 1998.*

7 | Apollinarius

It's not easy being a heretic. Ask any of the folks we've talked about in this series, they'll tell you—it's no piece of cake. It's painful to be cast aside by the very people who have cared for you, loved you, and built you up.

I remember when I was in high school, I was a leader in my youth group at Berea Baptist Church. I had a license to preach, and did so every Sunday afternoon on my high-school radio show, POWER-MUSIC. I would play rock-n-roll by Christian artists for an hour and a half and then I would preach for half an hour before I got in my car and sped back to church for choir practice and Sunday evening prayer meeting.

This worked fine for a while, until my youth pastor began to be influenced by "independent" Baptist theology as taught by Jack Hyles and Bob Jones, of the infamous Bob Jones University, which until a few years ago still expelled students for cross-racial dating. Not only did our youth pastor inform our interracial couples that they were no longer an item, but he also got the idea into his head that the 4/4 beat that most rock-n-roll is based on was demonic and irredeemable, the product of Satan-worshipping druids.

Never mind the simple historical fact that the druids had never heard of Satan, let alone worshipped him, or that the rock-n-roll

beat was derived more from African music than from the music of
the ancient Britons. The Beatles were branded the high priests of
Satanic druidry, and every secular record from Abba to Queen was
scrutinized for Satanic messages when played backwards.

Eventually our youth pastor hauled us all the way to Hammond,
Indiana in a van to attend one of Jack Hyle's youth rallies, and we
got turned on to this anti-rock-n-roll crusade ourselves. When I got
back, I was one confused puppy. I even put myself on a strict diet of
the Statler Brothers to see if I was under Satan's rock-n-roll control.
I lived through the week of Statler Brothers—although I still have an
irrational fear of four-part all-male harmony—but what really got me
was what happened when I announced to my father that I was quitting my radio show. Dad whipped around and fairly shrieked,
"What??"

"I'm quitting my radio show," I said again, less certain this time.
"Who says?" my Dad countered. So I told him all about what I had
learned from Jack Hyles and my youth pastor's new-found disdain
for electric guitars. "So, I thought," I finished, "that I should probably quit my show."

"Think again," Dad said, and he gave me a very serious speech on
blind faith, which I have always cherished. I have to admit, though,
it was confusing. I was being told that I should stand up for what I
believe is right even in the face of a religious authority figure who
disagreed with me. And I did. I informed my youth pastor that I
would not, in fact, be quitting my show.

And how did my youth pastor respond to this defiance? He
scheduled a special youth Bible study at exactly the same time as my
radio show (so that I conveniently could not attend), and at those
Bible studies began to indoctrinate the only friends I had in the
world against me. Thus, a couple of weeks later, when I showed up
after my radio show for choir practice, I felt a cold chill in the air
that I could not explain. None of my friends would speak to me, in
fact, none of them even made eye contact. I was beginning to get a
little weirded out when we stopped for a break. Everyone wandered
away from me except Ron, who I had always considered a little too
fickle to be a close friend. He looked me up and down like he was
appraising a spent mule, and finally pronounced his judgement.
"You know what you are, John? You're a druid. You listen to Satanic
druid music, and you're a druid. Druid, druid, druid."

That doesn't sound like such a bad thing to me now—I have a great deal of esteem for native Celtic religion, but at the time, I knew exactly what Ron meant by this, and I was crushed. Remember, I was a religious freak at this time, and had no friends outside of my youth group. And now, to a person, my pastor had turned them against me. I left that church the very next week and never went back.

Of course, I still talked to some of my old "friends," who would still speak to me privately, if not publicly. A couple of months later, when I heard that Ron had been run out of the youth group on a rail for being a homosexual, (I'm a little chagrined to admit to you) I beamed inside. He certainly had gotten his, I thought. Another great example of "what goes around comes around."

Another person who learned this lesson all too well was a bishop named Apollinarius in the middle fourth century. Apollinarius had been a big-wig at the Nicene Council, and in fact was Athanasius' right-hand man during the condemnation of the Arian heresy. It shouldn't surprise any of us that when witch-hunters have caught one witch, they begin casting about for another, but Apollinarius certainly did not expect the next witch to be him!

Sadly, it was; Apollinarius, who had fought so vehemently against the heresies of Arius, had become the next target of the early church's rabid heresy-hunters.

Not that it was really Apollinarius' fault. He was kind of set-up for heresy by the times he lived in, and the circles within which he moved. For as soon as the great trinitarian debates had been completed, and it was established that Jesus was fully God, fully eternal, fully omnipotent, the question had to be asked, "in exactly what part of Jesus did his Godhead reside?"

Apollinarius' answer was a heresy waiting to happen. Assuming, as most neo-Platonists did, that human beings were comprised of three parts, the body, the soul, and the spirit, it seemed logical to our good bishop that one of these was simply "replaced" in Jesus with the Logos. The body certainly wasn't replaced by the Logos, that was fully human, inherited from Mary. The soul was thought of as our lower, animal nature comprised mostly of our emotions and intuition, and this part, too, was deemed unlikely to have been replaced by the Logos, for it was not highly esteemed enough. But the highest part of human beings, the spirit, or in Greek terms, the intellect or psyche, surely that was the likeliest candidate. Thus, Apollinarius taught that Jesus had no human spirit, but that in place of his spirit, the Logos was in residence.

A neat-sounding answer to the problem, don't you think? Apollinarius did, and so did many bishops who agreed with him. Unfortunately for him, though, most of the bishops had grave reservations about his theory. The biggest problem they had was this: if Jesus did not have a human spirit, then how could we possibly say that Jesus was fully human? He would not be fully human, of course, but instead, some kind of weird half-breed.

Now human-divine half-breeds were common enough in the mythologies of the empire, and this may be exactly why the other bishops were so fiercely opposed to Apollinarius' theory: Jesus was no Hercules, nor anything like him or any of the other divine half-breeds of popular legend.

Another reason this would not have been acceptable is this: if Jesus was not fully human, he could not fully save humans. That sounds confusing, doesn't it? The propounder of this doctrine was Gregory Nazainzus, who said "God cannot save what God does not assume." Now, that's not much clearer, I know, but basically what he was trying to say was that God could only save that part of Creation into which God had fully and completely entered. It was through God's wedding of Godself with creation that the wounds of the Fall were healed. If there were any part of the Creation which God did not meld with, did not enter into, did not "assume," then that part could not be redeemed. Thus, according to Apollonarius' theory, the body and soul could be saved, since God fully melded with Jesus' body and soul, but the spirit could not, since Jesus did not have a human spirit for God to meld with.

And what, his opponents wanted to know, was the point of Jesus coming to save sinners, if he could not save their spirits? Worst of all, if Christ's intellect were identical with God's, then any idea about Jesus' being "tempted in all ways as we are" went completely out the window. Jesus' prayers in the Garden of Gethsemene would be a complete charade. Such a theory certainly protected Jesus from the ability to sin, but it also denied him any meaningful humanity, and came dangerously close to the Gnostic dismissal of Jesus as anything but simply a divine being. Some of Apollinarius' followers even went so far as to say that there was nothing human about Jesus except his flesh, and others went still further, claiming that even Jesus' flesh had been changed into pure divinity.

Even though his brother bishops condemned him, none of his rivals proposed anything quite so neat and tidy as his formulation. In fact, some of their conclusions were just plain nonsensical. David Christie-Murray tells us that, in fact, Diodorus, bishop of Tarsus, drew a sharp distinction between "the Son of God" and "the Son of Mary." Afraid that this distinction might be interpreted as a separation in the person of Jesus, he added, almost as an afterthought, "But there are not two Sons." Unfortunately, he does not attempt to explain this seeming contradiction.

Also, unfortunately, no answer was to be forthcoming for quite some time. "How do two natures go to make up one person?" was the $20,000 question amongst the bishops of the fourth century. As Apollinarius found out, trying to answer that question can get you into a heap of trouble.

So what are we to make of Apollinarius today? Certainly his Jesus is not very far afield from the Jesus many Christians worship today. Whenever I watch King of Kings or another of those films made of Jesus' life, it seems that they went and hired Apollinarius' Jesus to play the part. The Jesus on the screen seems to be just playing at this humanity thing in these movies. When he speaks, it is only in whispers, and everyone for miles around can miraculously hear him. People he doesn't know recognize him as God and fall at his feet. He somehow moves without ruffling his robes, and he is trailed by a faint halo.

"Pee-yoo," I always say when I finish one of those movies, and maybe you know what I mean. I'm sure that Apollinarius' fellow bishops would understand my reaction, for like them, I have little use for a Jesus who is not human.

But perhaps, like Apollinarius and his followers, you need a divine Jesus to lift you up, to know all that there is to know, to take the uncertainty out of this crazy life. If so, then I say "power to you." But I doubt whether such a Jesus is going to catch on, especially in this deconstructed day and age. But plenty of Christians do want a Jesus like this, and apparently, a number of film-makers do as well.

If there's one lesson to be learned from Apollinarius' experience, though, I think it would be this: be careful whom you choose as your friends, since fierce friends may quickly become fierce enemies.

I'm sure that Apollinarius only had the best of intentions proclaiming Arius a heretic, just as I'm sure my friend Ron felt he was entirely within his rights to proclaim me a druid. But as they both discovered, witch-hunters are always eager for new prey.

Holy and just God who put the stars into motion and formed the tenderness of our hearts with your fingers, you have told us "judge not lest we ourselves be judged" and yet you watch as, again and again, we condemn each other and wreck the most unspeakable cruelties upon our sisters and brothers in your own name. Help us to learn from your servant Apollinarius, who sought only a sensible faith, and was repaid with the same lack of compassion of which he himself was guilty. Speak to our hearts, and help us to heed his lesson, that we may continue to seek after a sensible faith, even as we seek to become living examples of your compassion. For we ask this in the name of the Human One, even Jesus Christ. Amen.

⊕ *Preached at Grace North Church October 18, 1998.*

8 | Nestorius

When I was growing up, the refrain that I often heard in church was, "Be careful of those Catholics, they worship idols!" My grandmother is especially suspicious of any sort of iconography, and unless the picture on your wall is a 1950's picture of Jesus holding a child in his lap, my grandmother is certain to disapprove. When I go down to L.A. to visit her, she will gladly accompany me to any evangelical bible bookstore I want to go to, but when I say I want to go to the bookstore nearest her house, she will most likely want to wait for me out in the car. It is a Catholic bookstore, you see, and I think all the little statues of Mary give her the creeps.

Well, she's not the only one. She would have gotten along just fine with the Nestorius, the fifth century patriarch of Constantinople. Nestorius was opinionated, tactless, rude, belligerent and manipulative, and his pushiness didn't make him any friends. He didn't care much about this when he was at the height of his power in the middle of the fifth century, as he was a merciless heresy hunter. He defeated the Arians, drove out the Novationists, and decimated the Quartodecimans. But just like Apollinarius before him, Nestorius did not see that his zeal would come back to bite him in the behind. This heresy hunter would also soon become the hunted.

It was easy to identify the gross heretics, those who said Jesus wasn't human, or that he didn't even have a real body—you know, stuff like that. But once those guys have been killed, the heresy hunters had to look closer and closer to home to find heretics. The teachings defined as heretical became pickier and pickier, and it became harder to actually figure out where they deviated from orthodox teaching. In fact, it almost takes a doctorate in theology to understand in what way Nestorius' teachings could actually be conceived of as heresy. Since we don't all have time or the inclination to do a doctoral program just to understand a subtle theological distinction, I will attempt to describe Nestorius' "heresy" in a simplistic and grossly inaccurate way in a sentence or two.

Nestorius, like so many heretics before him, was trying to describe exactly how it is that God was in Jesus. According to Nestorius, Jesus shares God's nature because he is God's Son, in the same way as I share human nature because my parents are human. Yet my parents and I are distinct beings. Nestorius kind of came to the same conclusion about God. God and Christ share the same nature, but they are distinct beings. Nestorius described their union as being similar to the union of a husband and wife. Two distinct beings, made one through a legal covenant.

So even though Nestorius said Jesus and God shared one nature, and were distinct persons, which none of his opponents disagreed with, the language he used implied that these two persons were two distinct beings, which his opponents could not tolerate, since, as the creed says, Jesus is "of one being with the father."

Confused yet? Just think of how theologically sophisticated we are today as compared to folks in the fifth century. Few people were educated at all, and if this distinction is difficult for us to fathom today, imagine trying to explain it to the average person in the street in Nestorius' time.

But it may be that none of this would have come down on Nestorius' head if he had not made so many enemies over "the Mary issue." Ever since the third century, it had been common to refer to the Virgin Mary as "Theotokos," or the Mother of God. Nestorius thought that this was a logical impossibility, for how could a fifteen-year-old girl give birth to a being older than she is? Nestorius also hated the statues of Mary circulating around, because it smacked to him of idolatry. Especially since it seemed that the statues were virtually identical to the statues of Isis and her baby son Horus, which had been popular for centuries. Folks just baptized their idols in Christian garb and kept right on worshipping them, and Nestorius wasn't going to stand for it.

Well, our poor bishop of Constantinople lost that round, and he lost the next one as well, since he was condemned in the year 431. Nestorius was exiled to Egypt, where he died in poverty and obscurity twenty years later in 451.

But that is not the end of the story, fortunately. Being the bishop of Constantinople is a *big* deal, kind of like being the pope of the East. Nestorius had a *lot* of bishops that agreed with his ideas, and when the council that condemned both them and Nestorius was over, though some of the bishops that sided with him recanted and were received back into "God's good graces," the bishops in Persia continued to stay true to Nestorius' formulation.

The Christians in Persia at that time lived as a minority religion in a country that was predominately Zoroastrian. Zoroastrianism teaches that there are two gods in the universe, a god of goodness and light, and a god of evil and darkness, and that these two gods are in a constant battle over the fate of the earth. The wise men who came to visit the baby Jesus were thought to be Zoroastrian priests, even by the Zoroastrians themselves. For when the Persians conquered the Holy Land in the early seventh century, they destroyed every church and shrine in Israel except for one: the Church of the Nativity in Bethlehem, where, not coincidentally, a mosaic of the three wise Zoroastrian sages was set over the door.

The effect that being Christians in a non-Christian country had on the Nestorians is that they were allowed to inculturate their religion to a far greater degree, now that the churches of the Roman empire were minding their own business. They really got the hang of translating their Christian faith into the idioms and traditions of the lands they happened to be living in, and this was a great boon to them in their strenuous missionary efforts in the seventh through ninth century.

Since the West was orthodox, the Nestorians turned towards the East. A missionary named Alopen was sent to evangelize the Chinese. Amazingly, Alopen was welcomed into the court of the Chinese emperor, who listened to Alopen with great interest. After all, to the Chinese, the West is the spiritual direction, so any spiritual teachers to come from the West, such as Buddha, and now Alopen, were given a good hearing, at least under the emperor Cheng-kuan. The emperor was so impressed with what came to be called "the shining teaching," that he ordered the Christian Sutras, or scriptures, to be translated immediately into Chinese.

And boy, did Alopen translate. The scriptures and other writings that Alopen produced were replete with Taoist and Buddhist imagery. In Alopen's works, Jesus didn't come to die for our sins, but to bring the great raft to rescue all beings from the suffering sin causes. Alopen had a genius for inculturating the gospel, for making the core teachings of Christianity understandable in the symbols and imagery of the country he was in. So successful was Alopen that soon there were Nestorian churches and monasteries in every province of China.

Unfortunately, not all of the emperors were so tolerant, and in the ninth century, all "foreign" religions, including Buddhism and Christianity, were outlawed. The churches were closed, and over 3,000 Nestorian monks were returned to regular life. Most of the monuments were destroyed, but some Nestorian crosses and one very significant artifact, the Nestorian Stone, still survive, along with many of Alopen's Sutras.

The Mongols to the North were among the various Chinese peoples evangelized, and history tells us that even Genghis Khan's mother was a Nestorian, along with many of his officers and soldiers. Christianity survived among the Mongols much longer than in the rest of China, and even as late as the thirteenth century two Mongolian priests set out from the cathedral in Peking with the blessing of Kublai Kahn. They visited Constantinople and Rome and even celebrated communion in the court of Edward the first in England.

Thus it was that this tiny pocket of heretics in Persia became one of the greatest missionary forces the world has ever known, and introduced to all of the East a form of Christianity that fit their culture, made sense to them, and continues to speak to us even today. Though most of the Nestorians were forcibly converted to Islam, there are still Nestorian churches in the East, some of whom have, ironically, kissed and made up with the Orthodox, realizing after fifteen hundred years, that their squabbles were pretty petty to begin with.

History is full of such ironies, but I have yet to tell you about the tastiest irony of all. It seems that before the Nestorians arrived in China, a minor deity of compassion was widely worshipped. His name was Quan-Yin, and the missionaries would have encountered countless shrines to this deity on their journeys. But human nature is hard to shake, you know, and even though Nestorius hated the little statues of the Virgin Mary, his own monks still clung to them, and carried them with them into China.

Isn't it odd, then, that after only a couple hundred years, Quan-Yin, deity of compassion, came to be known as a female deity, rather than male, and amazingly, her later statues showed her cradling a child in her lap, almost identical to Isis and Horus, or Mary and Jesus. Quan-Yin is still a popular figure even today. In fact, rarely a week goes by that I don't see a statue of her right here in Berkeley.

Funny how these things come around, don't they? So what is it we can learn from the Nestorians? First, perhaps, do unto others as you would have them do unto you. If Nestorius had followed that simple scriptural admonition, his end may have been much different indeed. But a much more positive lesson comes to us from his followers, who understood that the good news of Jesus can be translated into any language, any culture. Unlike Western missionaries, who reviled the local cultures and insisted that converts become experts in Western philosophy and theology, the Nestorians showed us the kind of power that good news can have when it is allowed to be spoken in people's native tongues.

For not only were the Chinese taught by Alopen's sutras, we Western Christians can be instructed as well, as we are fortunate enough to be given the gift of seeing the good news through fresh eyes. For while we all know that Jesus came to save sinners—and yes, feel free to yawn as you say it—it can be quite a revelation to us to hear that Jesus came to liberate all beings from suffering. It is no less true than the first statement, but it is not the same old thing, it can catch us off guard, and help us to see the greatest story ever told in ways that are vibrant, fresh, and infused with the power to impart life to all those who have ears to hear.

God of all the earth, you have said that there is nothing new under the sun. And indeed, there is nothing of Nestorius' story that is unfamiliar to us today. The heresy hunters are still sharpening their blades, and true believers of every stripe continue to argue and tear each other down. Help us to open our eyes to the universality of your gospel. Help us to recognize you in whatever form you take. Help us to cling to the essence of what you are, and leave the nit-picky details to those who have nothing better to do. But to us you have given much work, and a great responsibility, to speak your good news in ways that can surprise, in images that people can understand, in forms that good people of faith everywhere can take to their hearts. For you are the giver of life, across all space and time, a holy trinity, of bliss, compassion, and liberation for all peoples. Amen.

⊕ *Preached at Grace North Church June 25, 2000.*

9 | The Monophysites

W hen I was growing up in the sixties, my mother was something of an Elvis freak. Now, one can hardly blame her. It *was* her turn to be an impressionable, screaming teenager when the country boy from Memphis, Tennessee was shaking his hips coast to coast on the Ed Sullivan Show. Being as how my mother was only eighteen when I was born, it's no surprise that I had heavy exposure to Elvismania in my formative years.

From the time I could figure out how to operate the turntable, I was spinning '45s by the King. I especially remember "Love Me Tender," "You Saw Me Crying in the Chapel," and of course the New Orleans-jazz tinged "Frankie and Johnny."

I have fond memories of standing on Mom's feet while she danced us around the room. They were good times, but they didn't stay that way. I also remember my mother's anguish as she watched as her idol was transformed from the lithe rockabilly star to the bloated has-been resting on his laurels in Vegas in the '70s.

When he finally died in the latter part of that decade, she was devastated. Idols, sadly, are destined to fall, and Elvis was no exception. But his untimely passing caused many to wonder where that fresh-faced young man from Memphis had gone to.

After all, we would not have elevated him to the status of "King of Rock-n-Roll" if he had not been one of *us*, the *hoi polloi*, the common folk. His right of ascension depended not on birthright or privilege, but on his own native chutzpah. Only because he was of the people could he possibly lead, affect, and inspire countless teenagers to swoon.

His meteoric rise and tragic fall forced us to consider the question: you can take the boy out of the country, but can you take the country out of the boy? Was the country boy utterly swallowed up by "the King"?

Now you might think this a bit of a stretch, but hang in there with me; I submit to you that it was a similar question that was being considered by the Christians of the fifth century regarding Jesus. Was Jesus really and truly one of us? Was he utterly flesh of our flesh, bone of our bone, or was whatever there was of humanity in him swallowed up by that part of him that was divine?

If you will recall our last sermon, the Nestorians were declared heretical because they put too much emphasis on Jesus' humanity. In the Nestorian view, Jesus' humanness was utterly intact, and he participated in the life of God through his familial relationship with the Father. Jesus possessed two distinct natures within him, a divine nature related to the Father, and a human nature, related by blood to the whole of the human race.

Of course, anyone who knows their Hegel will tell you that any thesis begets an antithesis, and in this case, the antithesis was known as "Monophysitism," or the assertion that there was in Christ not two natures, but one, and that one was wholly divine.

It started with a cantankerous monk named Eutyches, the abbot of a large monestary in Constantinople. Eutyches was a fierce opponent of Nestorianism, and as is often the case with zealots, he saw them pesky Nestorian demons everywhere. Especially in his fellow churchmen who paid attention to Jesus' humanity.

Specifically, Eutyches formulated his Christology as follows: Jesus was *of* two natures, but not *in* them. Before the incarnation there were two separate natures, divine and human, but after Jesus' birth his human nature was swallowed up by his divinity, until ultimately it was only his godhood that mattered.

Of two natures, but not *in* them? This war of prepositions sounded as ludicrous to his opponents as they do to us today, but Eutyches stuck to his guns, insisting that Jesus was of one nature with the father, but was not of one nature with humanity.

The orthodox could not stand for this, of course, and they deposed him and gave him the title "reviler of Christ," which, as scholar David Christie-Murray points out, is "scarcely a fair description of one who had over-emphasized the Lord's divinity" (69).

But theologically, the orthodox made a good case. If Jesus was not fully human, he could not take humanity into the godhead. If Jesus was not fully human, he could not be Paul's "second Adam." If Jesus was not fully human, then his crucifixion and resurrection were a masquerade, and no more salvific than the exploits of Mithra or Apollo. If he were not one of *us*, he could not save us.

But Eutyches had friends in high places, and the emperor was persuaded to call a council to reopen the matter. Held in the year 449, its ranks were packed with Eutyches' supporters, and legates from the Pope were not even allowed a hearing. The council came to be known as the *Latrocinium*, or in English, the Robber Council. It was a kangaroo court in every way. Not only did it restore Eutyches, but it barred the orthodox emperor from observing its deliberations, declared everyone who opposed them Nestorian heretics, and even excommunicated the Pope. Eutyches, you ain't nothin' but a hound dog, you scoundrel you.

This ruling could not stand, of course, and in a short time, Pope Leo called another council which repealed the Robber Council's decisions and declared Eutyches and all who followed him heretics.

Not that that mattered much to those who followed Eutyches. They simply formed their own church, and the Monophysite churches began their life as a religion separate from the orthodox, flourishing mostly in the East, away from the long arm of imperial law.

But just because the majority of Monophysites went off and formed their own churches, it did not mean that the monophysite position was entirely dead in the orthodox churches. As the orthodox clung tenaciously to a delicate tightrope walk between Jesus' humanity and divinity, there would always be those who leaned further in one direction or the other, and thus the teaching would rear its head again and again, and indeed, remains with us even today.

One teaching, put forward by Patriarch Sergius of Constantinople in the year 634 was known as "monoenergism," which stated that Christ worked both human and divine deeds through one divine-human operation, or *energia*. This view gained some popularity, and in fact, one of the most profound works of Christian mysticism that we have, the works of Pseudo-Dionysius, are Monoenergistic in theology. Since there is hardly a seminarian in the country that does not have to study Pseudo-Dionysius, this history is important.

Another form of this heresy, known as Monotheletism, arose in an attempt to bridge the two factions that remained in the orthodox church. This position stated that though there were two natures in Christ, there was only one will, the will of God. This theory gained wide acceptance, and the emporer Hereclitus pushed this position hard, since he was desperate to show the invading Muslims a united front.

But to Heraclitus' dismay, the Pope would not play ball. Pope Severinus declared that Jesus, in fact, possessed two wills, one human and one divine. But, Severinus insisted, those two wills were *always* in agreement. Yeah, okay…. But apparently that didn't sound quite so ridiculous then as it does now, and Severinus' declaration carried the day. But that was not the end of the story.

The emperor Constans II in the year 648 found himself in quite a pickle. In only fifteen years, the Muslims had taken from him Damascus, Antioch, Jerusalem, all of Mesopotamia, Alexandria, and the whole of North Africa, and much much more. He forbade the discussion of "energies" or "wills." But the new Pope, Martin, continued harping on the "two wills" theory. So the emperor had Pope Martin stripped, led through the city in an iron collar, imprisoned, and finally exiled.

Finally, at the sixth Ecumenical Council in the seventh century, both Monoenergism and Monotheletism were condemned once and for all.

But the Monophysite churches are still with us. Largely due to the efforts of a curious character named James the Ragged, who reportedly ordained over a hundred thousand Monophysite priests and organized what would later be called the Jacobite churches with a central authority and a structure much like the orthodox churches.

And though they have met with great persecution throughout the years, the Jacobite churches are still with us. The Coptic Orthodox church of Egypt is monophysite, as is the Armenian Orthodox Church, and the Orthodox Church of Ethiopia. Unlike so many other heresies, this one has a happy ending. In 1984 the Jacobite churches were able to settle their differences with the orthodox

churches, and submitted to the authoriy of the Ecumenical patriarch, the "pope" of the Eastern Orthodox churches.

What can we learn from the Monophysites' tribulations? For one
thing, they are evidence of what a difficult struggle it can be to hold
humanity and divinity in tension. This struggle divided families,
destroyed careers, and almost tore an empire apart. Jesus, the orthodox had decided, was both fully human *and* fully divine, and this
impossible tension was to be maintained at all costs.

But it is difficult to live in tension. If Jesus' humanity was not completely engulfed by his godhood, then Jesus must have suffered terribly with this division inside himself. This painful split is the subject of
Nikos Kazantzakis' compelling novel *The Last Temptation of Christ.*

And though Jesus has super-human strength to call upon to survive his internal struggle, not all kings are so lucky, especially if you
are the King of Rock-n-Roll.

Which brings us back to my original question: did the King finally obliterate the country boy? I have to come down on the side of the
orthodox, here.

I believe that being Elvis the King did not, ultimately, swallow up
Elvis the country boy. The crown would not have been so ill-fitting,
the fame would not have been so hard to handle, or his demons so
fierce had he not, at his core, been a fish out of water. He was the
pauper living the life of the prince; he was not born for it, and it
never really suited him. He was a country boy to the end, and in the
end, it was precisely this discrepancy that killed him.

It is hard to be a walking contradiction, and whether you are the
King of Rock or the King of Kings, it is not an enviable position.

*Jesus, you are God, and you show us God. Inspire us as your body to
show God to those around us, and to be especially gracious and loving to
those with whom we disagree, about theology, politics, or even manners.
Jesus, you are human, and you show us what it is like to be whole. Inspire
us to likewise strive for wholeness, and to assist others in their healing.
Help us to embrace the contradiction that is you, and in so doing, to reconcile the angelic and demonic forces within ourselves. For you are the
coincidence of opposites, the walking contradiction that bids us to pick up
our beds, and walk beside you. Amen.*

⊕ *Preached at Grace North Church July 16, 2000.*

10 | Pelagius

Last week I was sitting in the Original Mel's Diner on Shattuck Avenue in Berkeley with a couple of friends, and we had murder on our minds. We had just finished watching the Coen brothers' amazing first film, *Blood Simple*, and were still kind of reeling from its hairpin plot twists and pessimistic portrayal of human nature. So I wasn't at all surprised when my friend Jon leaned across the table dangerously and said, "If you could off one person in history, who would it be?"

Our other companion and I said, almost together, "You mean, besides Hitler?"

"Yes," he said, "Besides Hitler, who is the one person in history you'd take out a contract on?"

Now, history is long, and I suppose a prudent person, even if he were to agree to such a shady proposition, would want to take his or her time to make the most of this intriguing hypothetical offer. But not me. Without hesitating a beat, I blurted out "St. Augustine." And I meant it.

"Egad!" You might be saying, "Fr. John would actually bump off a saint?" Horrifying, isn't it? And yet, I believe the evil wrought by the teachings of this one theologian give even Hitler a run for his money. So, horrifying as it might be to actually speak it aloud, I have to affirm that yes, given the chance, I would gladly erase Augustine from history.

I don't think I'm alone. In the fifth century, a quiet monk from Wales named Pelagius and many of his supporters may very well have felt similarly, and may indeed have requested a viewing at Augustine's hypothetical execution.

The root of Pelagius' dispute with Augustine is really a philosophical difference of opinion between theologians in the East and theologians in the West. In the fourth century the great doctor of the church, St. John Chrysostom, preached that human beings have free will, and when people choose to do good, God sends his grace to assist them in that good. At the same time, St. Ambrose in the West was teaching that all humans were tainted by the sin of Adam, and incapable of doing good of our own acord. The question this ultimately comes down to is this: is human nautre intrinsically good or intrinsically evil?

This philosophical split continues to this day. In the West, when we say we believe in "original sin" we are still following in Ambrose's theological footsteps. "Original sin" in the West means that Adam's sin is passed down genetically from father to children. In other words, in the West we are born bad and just get worse.

The Eastern Orthodox church, by contrast, calls the Western formulation "original guilt." The Orthodox still teach what they call "original sin" but they mean something very different by it than we do. In the East this phrase refers to the sin in human society which so quickly corrupts the innocent. Human beings are born with a tendancy to fall into error, but they are not born with the stain of sin from the word "go."

The East and West had so many Christological disputes that they didn't really lock horns on the human nature issue. But it really came to a head when this plucky monk from the West started parroting very Eastern-sounding doctrines.

Understand that Pelagius was far from a charismatic individual. He wasn't particularly spectacular in any way. He wasn't a gifted theologian; he wasn't a stunning orator. What he was was a dedicated monk, an eminently respectable individual incapable of either great sin or unusual virtue. He controlled his appetites, followed a strict ascetic discipline, and believed that God would reward him for his efforts.

All humans, he believed, could live upright lives before God if they chose to. If they tried hard enough, they could even achieve sinlessness, and even be fit for heaven, all by their own efforts. Unlikely, perhaps, but it could happen.

All human beings come into the world with a clean slate, Pelagius taught. And if they were properly trained and chose to work hard enough on their own moral development, they could live blameless lives before God. Even sinners can turn over a new leaf if they choose to. People have free will, Pelagius taught, and can choose good or ill of their own accord.

In the early fifth century, Pelagius had travelled to Rome and was held in high esteem in that city for his virtuousness and his teaching. But when Rome fell in 410 CE, many Christians fled to Egypt, Pelagius among them. Fatefully, a disciple of Ambrose named Augustine was there to meet him. Augustine initially wrote favorably of Pelagius' great sanctity, but then Pelagius started teaching in his new home. And Augustine was horrified by what he heard.

You see, Pelagius and Augustine were of totally opposite natures. Pelagius was quiet, controlled, and decent. Virtue came easy to this easy-going guy. But Augustine was a very different sort of fellow. Augustine was a hell-raiser who could only go all the way in one direction or another. Augustine was a man for whom the word "moderation" did not exist. He was either causing trouble or writing against it. The man was always out of control, and he was either out-of-control sinning or he was out-of-control punishing himself for his sinful nature.

The problem with human beings is that we somehow assume that on some fundamental level, all people are just like we are. I am an artist and so I assume that everybody has a spark of creativity in them ready and waiting to leap out. Augustine was a borderline personality who simply assumed that everyone on earth was the same degree of hellion that he was, and of course Pelagius thought that everyone could control themselves if they wanted to, just like he did. I think you will agree that people are different, and Pelagius and Augustine were both blowing smoke, here.

But Augustine was not a man to let his passions be ruled by his reason, no matter how neurotically saintly he was driven to be, and in 416 he called a council of bishops to condemn Pelagius of heresy.

Pelagius said that babies were born sinless. Augustine countered that the little beasts were "the very limbs of Satan," and that's a quote. Pelagius said that humans had free will, and could choose to do good or evil. Augustine countered that no one has free will, but instead was predestined for either heaven or hell and there wasn't a darn thing a person could do about it one way or the other.

Augustine had many more friends in high places than Pelagius did, and not surprisingly, the council condemned Pelagius, and sent a report to Pope Innocent III. The report erroneously read that Pelagius denied the importance of infant baptism or petitionary prayer, for which errors Pope Innocent felt compelled to condemn him. The irony is that both of these issues were caricatures, and not representative of Pelagius' teaching at all.

Pelagius did not simply roll over and die, I'm happy to report. He rallied support, and miraculously Pope Innocent died just weeks after signing Pelagius' condemnation. The next Pope, Zosimus, was sympathetic to Pelagius' ideas, and dismissed Innocent's condemnation, rightly stating that the condemnation was based on an erroneous presentation of Pelagius' ideas.

Not to be undone, Augustine then wrote to the Eastern Churches, so cleverly presenting Pelagius' "heresy" that even these bishops who *agreed* with Pelagius' positions on free will and original sin condemned him. Finally Pope Zosimus folded under the pressure, and Pelagius was declared a heretic once and for all. He was exiled to the desert, where he died two short years later.

And what about Augustine? Well, he went on to become one of the most influential theologians the West has ever known. He almost single-handedly brought the gnostic Manichean heresy into the church, and due to his powerful connections, made it the official teaching of the Western church. Thus, ever since Augustine, we have viewed the body as evil and the spirit as good; women as evil and men as good. Augustine taught in fact that women were worse than cesspools and were the agents of Satan hell-bent on corrupting the souls of men. Augustine taught that when the evil angels fell out of heaven, they left only a certain number of spaces to be filled by the "elect." Everyone else is condemned to an everlasting hellfire, which, according to Augustine, we all deserve anyway, so stop yer belly-aching!

There's no question Augustine's God was a monster who does not deserve our loyalty, and certainly not our love. And since we all strive to be like our ideals, Augustine was quite a little monster himself, whose theological horrors we have yet to live down even to this very day.

But even though Pelagius died a lonely death in the desert, the world did not hear the last of his ideas. Much later Arminius would oppose Calvin on the very same questions of predestination, and like Pelagius, Armenian theology holds fast to the notion that human beings are free to choose good or evil.

It may be that some of Pelagius' teaching was tied to his British soil, since many of his ideas would pop up again and again on the green islands. The Puritans believed that through self-discipline and hard work, a person may live a spotless life before God, and they actively sought to do so. The Wesleys, likewise, taught a doctrine of holiness that has its roots in the theology of their ancient countryman, Pelagius.

Now, do I agree with all of Pelagius' ideas? Heck, I'm not sure I agree with everything I say to you day in and day out. Human beings are fickle folk, even—or perhaps especially—when it comes to the realm of ideas. Sure, some of his ideas may be dangerous if taken to their extreme conclusions. But were they more dangerous than Augustine's harebrained notions? Not by a longshot.

It is my firm belief that the history of the world would have been much better off if it had been Augustine who had been condemned and exiled to the desert instead of Pelagius. Oh, sure, it's not as dramatic as sending him to the electric chair, but perhaps that's overkill. I would be content indeed to know that Augustine had just wandered off into the desert and died. Who knows? Perhaps he might have been eaten by lions. After all, I can dream, can't I?

Augustine, what were you thinking? It is my solemn hope that when you reached the gates of glory you may have discovered that your neuroses were not shared by everybody, and not everybody is simply born bad. I wonder if you and Pelagius have settled your differences, and embraced one another as brothers? I must hope that such reconciliations are possible. And I am sorry for saying I would want you offed. I think, more than anything, I would simply like to hear you say you're sorry, not just for what you did to our pal Pelagius, but to all of us down through the ages upon whom your eccentric and frankly pathological notions have been foisted: the generations of women who were abused for being "Satan's agents," the countless sensitive souls who committed suicide because they saw themselves as sinful and stained beyond redemption. Intercede with us, Augustine, and pray for us here on earth, that we may resist such poisonous theologies and embrace ourselves and one another as the beloved children of God that we all—all—are. Amen.

⊕ *Preached at Grace North Church July 30, 2000.*

11 | John Scotus Eriugena

Several years ago, I was watching television with my ex-wife, Cherrisa. It was, if I recall rightly, an episode of *Hill Street Blues*, back when that august program was still running in prime time. I was delighted by the writing on this particular episode, and was so busy supplying a theological explication of the action that it was impossible for Cherrisa to hear the dialogue. Finally, in a fit of exasperation, she snapped at me, "Damn it, John, everything is not about God!"

I remember that moment as clearly as if it was yesterday, and I also remember my response. "Well," I said, "I beg to differ. Everything *is* about God, if you only have the eyes to see it."

Cherrisa basically told me to shut up and stop being a pompous ass. I don't remember if I sulked for the rest of the program, but knowing me, I probably did.

Still, I don't feel any differently after all this time. Everything to me *is* about God, and call me a dreamer, but most of my days are rather extended meditations on this theme, looking for glimmers of the divine in the most unlikely places as I go about my daily business.

A man after my own heart in this regard was a Celtic scholar named John Scotus Eriugena, who lived in the ninth century. His name is redundant, since it literally means John the Scotsman, the

Irishman. Since Ireland was at this time considered Scotland major, and Scotland as we know it Scotland minor, his name is not so great a contradiction as it first appears. In fact, it seems that he invented the name Eriugena himself while translating the works of Pseudo-Dionysius.

Though he was born in Ireland, political situations drove him to Paris, where he was a celebrated teacher and theologian. Since he left a couple of sermons behind, it is likely that he was a deacon, though probably not a priest, as no record of his being such survives.

In Paris he was court theologian to the Holy Roman Emperor Charles the Bald, who was also his patron and friend. Eriugena was called upon many times to give his opinions on important theological matters, including the ongoing debate about predestination.

Eriugena's approach was rational. In fact, he was a formidable logician, as any student of his works will attest with some dismay. His logic is impeccable but not necessarily easy to follow. A couple of years of algebra help enormously when approaching his work. As numbers and I are not on speaking terms, I'll try to give you the gist of it, if not the particulars.

If John had been a Hindu, he would have followed the path of *jñana* yoga, the spiritual path of knowledge, for he believed that philosophy is the only way to salvation. He advocated the internal authority of one's own reason, which you might expect would put him at odds with the external authority of the church, but he articulated his position with subtlety. He taught that since the ways of God were ultimately rational, it is impossible for true reason to contradict legitimate authority.

Reason is also congruent with nature. Not unlike another John watching television a thousand years later, John Eriugena taught that everything in nature is a kind of sign of something spiritual, and that reason can detect these correspondences. In other words, yes, Cherrisa, everything *is* about God. Just as Aquinas would later refer to the two forms of God's self-revelation as the book of scripture and the book of nature, so Eriugena said that the Word walks with two feet: nature and scripture. And if rightly discerned, the two cannot contradict one another.

And just as religious conservatives today speak of "rightly dividing the word of truth," so Eriugena was concerned with properly dividing the revelation of nature. It is, in fact, in this division that he shines so brightly. For John Eriugena, nature could be divided into two axes, which form the familiar image of the celtic cross.

The first division of nature is that which creates but is not created—in other words, God as the starting point of all things.

The second axis is that which is created and also itself creates—into this category, Eriugena puts the Platonic forms: love, beauty, truth, and so on. These forms impact themselves upon matter, much as we say "the word became flesh."

The third division of nature is that which is created, but does not itself create. Into this category he placed the sensible world, including humans and other animals.

The fourth and final axis is that which is not created and does not create, or God as Omega point of all creation.

The truly amazing thing about this quadrilateral is that two of the four poles are reserved for God "himself." In other words, Eriugena has yanked God out of the sky and made him an integral and inseperable part of nature. God is not beyond nature, but instead the greater part of it.

Since both time and space are created entities, God is at once beyond them and contains them. All time occurs simultaneously to God, all space is contained within God. God is no time, and God is no *where*, since all whens and wheres are present to him at once. Since God is a nothing, or a *no-thing*, we can speak of all things being created *ex nihilo*, out of nothing.

The amazing conclusion we come to here is that there is no room for the supernatural in John's system. God is natural, is part and parcel of nature, not separate from it.

Now, since God is not a being, we cannot understand God. But even more amazingly, Eriugena says that God does not understand Godself! Creation is a divine experiment, a mirror in which God hopes to glimpse himself and thereby come to know Godself. As one philosopher notes: "God does not understand himself. But he is not ignorant of himself, if by that we mean that there is something he doesn't know about himself. He simply doesn't know what he is, since he isn't a 'what' at all" (*De Mirabilibus Mundi*).

Now if this sounds neo-Platonic, it is. And if it sounds to you that his position smacks of Gnosticism, in which the Creation and the Fall are one and the same necessary event, you would be correct, since the fall must occur so that God can come to a saving knowledge of himself. Do you see the irony in this system? In orthodox Christianity, God in Christ sacrifices Godself for the salvation of humankind. But in Eriugena's system, humankind is sacrificed so that God may be saved.

Humankind exists as a Platonic ideal in the second division of nature, what we might call the "mind" of God. When Adam sinned, humankind fell short of that ideal, unfortunately and inexplicably dragging all of the created order with us. Now this is not much different from the teaching of the Eastern Orthodox churches, in which all of nature began its devolution with Adam's Fall.

For the Orthodox, salvation occurs when humankind is divinized, or taken into God via the power of the Resurrection. In the Resurrection, the devolution of the universe is halted, and evolution and the slow process of the divinization of the universe is begun. Likewise in John's system, the process of divinization will continue until all of nature is reabsorbed into the undifferentiated unity of God.

And because all things will eventually be reconciled and reabsorbed into divinity, Eriugena denied the existence of Satan as an actual being; it is simply not logical that such a being could exist as a part of God. By extension, all evil in his system is ultimately illusory. It is the result of human choices, and since all humans, and indeed, all of nature will one day be reabsorbed into divinity, our bad choices and the evil we perceive will one day pass like waking from a bad dream.

John was not without his opponents. His views were denounced by two local councils, and his writings were declared anathema by the church at large three centuries later. But he was never removed from his post or excommunicated. His most vicious naysayers, in fact, were his students. Now maybe it was his outrageous teaching that angered them, or maybe he simply refused to grade on a curve. Whatever the reason, legend has it that one day his students became so incensed that they rose up and stabbed him to death with their quill pens.

Is John Eriugena a heretic? I suppose it depends upon your perspective. He was formally denounced not for his views on God, or nature, or even because his system smacks of pantheism, but because he strongly defended the position that human beings have free will, that God's knowledge of all time and space does not relieve human beings of their responsibility, that human action is important and possesses ultimate meaning.

Surely there are few of us who would quibble with this position today. And though some of his theologizing might sound exotic to us, it is not strange when placed alongside other famous neo-Platonic theologians such as Origen, Gregory of Nyssa, or Pseudo-Dionysius.

What was unusual is that during the West's darkest days, in which the Holy Roman Empire found itself sunk into one of the bleakest periods of ignorance and violence, so great a light was allowed to shine at all. And that so much of his work survives after his being declared a heretic is likewise amazing. It is also our great good fortune, for in John Eriugena we find the seeds that would flower in later thinkers such as Nicolas of Cusa and Meister Eckhardt, from whom we will hear more in a later sermon.

John affords us an amazing model with which to view God, one which presages the process theology of Alfred North Whitehead, and gives a rational basis for the truth that has been known intuitively by mystics of every tradition: that all of nature is charged with the grandeur of God. That creation and creator are inseparable partners in the great dance of time, that from God all things emerge, and into God all things must eventually return.

God of all time and space, in whom we live, move, and have our being; teach us not to fear the gift of pure reason, help us to see your footprints in the sands of earth, and to discern your wisdom in every creature. For our beginning is in you, and our end is in you, Alpha and Omega. Amen.

⊕ *Preached at Grace North Church August 20, 2000.*

12 | Peter Abelard

In preparation for this sermon, I not only scoured many books, but also went in search of a film I had seen a little over ten years ago, titled *Stealing Heaven*, which is a drama portraying the relationship between Abelard and his great love Heloise. Walking in to a video store, I decided the quickest way to discern whether the video was in stock was to inquire at the desk. I was quite surprised when the clerk on duty directed me to the Erotic Film section. "Are you sure?" I asked. "Only movie called 'Stealing Heaven' we have, dude," he replied. I quickly glanced around to see if anyone that mattered might see me making for the Erotic Film section. But I remembered what Martin Luther had said, "If you are going to sin, sin boldly." Boldly, then, I marched to the Erotic Film section. And sure enough, nestled in between *Playboy Bunnies in the Snow* and the *Red Shoe Diaries* was a purple video with a steamy scene on the front cover; a cover which read "Stealing Heaven." I mused on the irony of finding a religious video in the Erotic Film section and I wondered whether perhaps I had misremembered the film.

Well, it was a good deal steamier than I remembered. This may be due to the fact that the copy this particular video store had was the unreleased "director's cut." Definitely not fare for your average religious prude. Not being much of a prude myself, I loved the film, and it seemed to be the perfect jumping off point for understanding the complex and intimate relationship between these two extraordinary individuals.

Even though Martin Luther lived nearly five hundred years after Abelard, our hero for the day would have appreciated and agreed with his words about sinning boldly. Abelard did not in fact shrink from acknowledging his own transgressions, and made them with full and conscious intent. Abelard was a man of passion who did nothing halfway. Even when he sinned, he went all the way, in more ways than one.

Peter Abelard was, first and foremost, a brilliant philosopher. Born in the late eleventh century, he was well-studied in the sciences and philosophy, and there wasn't a teacher in the land who could touch him. Partly this was because of his formidable native talent for debate, but it was also because he wasn't afraid to push the boundaries and even sin if it got him what he wanted.

As far as philosophy goes, this means he willingly thought "outside the box," even though he knew he was risking damnation to do so. Since none of his teachers were willing to make such a sacrifice, he had an astounding edge on them in that he permitted himself to think creatively when it came to theological and philosophical questions. If the dictionary definition of a heretic is "one who questions"—and that *is* the dictionary definition—then Abelard is the very platonic ideal of the heretic. He dared to question because he saw that only through questioning may the truth be discerned. And he was certainly more interested in truth than in dogma.

He was a wild bachelor-teacher, arrogant about his intellectual prowess, and what he himself refers to as his "exceptional good looks." Abelard says of himself, "I possessed such advantages of youth and comeliness, that no matter what woman I might favor with my love, I dreaded the rejection of none."

By incredible good fortune, Abelard had scored quite a *coup* by winning for himself a coveted chair at the cathedral school in Paris. He was the envy of all the other teachers, dangerously so, as it turns out. But in fact, Abelard's greatest enemy would turn out to be his own formidable passions, for he soon spied the niece of the cathedral's canon, and fell instantly and head over heels in love with her. It was, of course, Heloise, who had encountered no little bit of trouble herself because of her own sharp intellect. It may be fair to say that she was Abelard's equal in many ways: she was certainly one of the most educated women in Europe, and the closest to being his intellectual peer that Abelard had ever encountered. Thus he says of her, "Of no mean beauty, she stood out above all by reason of her abundant knowledge of letters."

A woman with a good body was of little interest to a man so ambitious as Abelard, but a woman with a good mind? Now that was a rare treasure indeed in the Dark Ages. Abelard says that he set about pursuing her as a hunter does his prey. He made a deal with her uncle that he would tutor her in exchange for lodgings in their house. For the canon, this was a deal he simply couldn't pass up. To have the honor of hosting the most acclaimed professor of the age, and to have him teach his niece to boot! He immediately agreed, and Abelard had gained his opening. Abelard spends a lot of time in his memoirs recounting how he tricked Heloise's uncle, but almost no time describing his seduction of her. He leaps almost immediately from gaining entrance to her house to gaining her love, as if winning her was the easiest part of his plan.

Well, perhaps it was. Abelard says, "Our speech was more of love than of the books which lay open before us; our kisses far outnumbered our reasoned words. Our hands sought less the book than each others' bosoms—love drew our eyes together far more than the lesson drew them to the pages of our text."

"Now, what is so bad about that?" You might be asking, "was he a priest or something?" Well, no. But he was a teacher, and even up until a hundred years ago professors were required to be celibate, as family life tended to distract one from one's books. So Abelard snuck around. They got away with it at first, but then, indeed, Abelard's teaching began to suffer. He started to rest on his laurels a little, and his students began to be suspicious. People began to talk. And of course, they talked to Heloise's uncle, who at first refused to believe it could be possible. But finally, he could ignore the signs no longer, and his grief was overwhelming.

Abelard stayed away for a while, but then he received a joyous letter from Heloise. She was pregnant, and wanted to know what Abelard would have her do. So one night while her uncle was away, Heloise and Abelard ran away to the house of Abelard's sister. While she was with child, Abelard returned to Paris and once more established himself as the greatest teacher of his age. When her uncle returned, Abelard went to see him, and asked both his forgiveness and Heloise' hand in marriage. Of course this meant giving up his greatest love: teaching philosophy. But even though Heloise tried, she could not dissuade him from his intent to marry her. And so in a private ceremony attended only by her uncle and some of Abelard's closest students, they were wed. Heloise then returned to Abelard's sister's house, where she stayed until the baby was born. They named the child "Astrolab" after an instrument that mapped the heavens.

Although Heloise's uncle seemed to be appeased, he was only biding his time until he could exact his revenge. And indeed, not long after, under the cover of night, he did. Bribing Abelard's servant, thugs hired by the canon gained access to the secret sleeping chamber in which Abelard had taken to hiding himself every night. It was a rude awakening indeed, as several of the men held him down, and one, wielding a sharp blade, castrated him.

Abelard is quite clear on the fact that when they made that cut, they took nearly everything. But, he says, the shame that was visited upon his soul was far greater than the pain borne by his body. He was convinced that his misfortune was well deserved and God's punishment upon him just. He and Heloise agreed that they would both enter monastic life, and leave Astrolab to be raised by Abelard's sister.

So Abelard went to the monastery and took to teaching theology, which he had not really studied very much and was most unqualified to teach. And yet it was that very ignorance of how theological issues had been handled in the past that freed him to come up with his own extremely creative solutions. As you might expect, these were not always well received. Abelard bounced from monastery to monastery for some time, for he always seemed to be in hot water with his superiors. Are we surprised? Of course not.

One of the doctrines which Abelard criticized was the theory of the atonement. Augustine taught that Jesus' crucifixion was the payment God offered to the devil in exchange for the souls of humankind. Since, when a man sins, he becomes the devil's property, Jesus provided the ransom to "buy back" humanity from Satan's clutches. St. Anselm, who died when Abelard was only thirty, provided another theory, one based on feudalism. Anselm held that Christ's death could not be a ransom to the devil because the devil was a usurper of God's power who had no legitimate claim on the human soul. Instead, he said, human sin besmirches God's honor, and in order for God to "save face" and maintain his honor, justice must be had for sin. In Anselm's system, God is a feudal lord whose honor has been maligned by uppity underlings, and in Jesus God is provided the scapegoat to satisfy the justice his honor demands.

This absurd feudal reading of the atonement is, inexplicably, the one that caught on in the West, and is generally accepted by both the Roman Church and most Protestant churches as well, especially evangelical churches, even though we no longer live in a feudal society, and even though we often ridicule cultures such as the Japanese or Chinese in which "saving face" is such an all-important consideration.

Instead, Abelard held that God has already forgiven humankind. The cross for Abelard was not a sacrifice to pay some price for sin, but instead it was a demonstration of God's love, that he has wedded himself to humankind, even unto death. The only thing Jesus' death does for us, Abelard said, was that by such an example "our hearts should be enflamed by such a gift of divine grace and true love," that we would do anything to see that this kind of injustice could not occur again, that our hearts would be reformed, and that we would be made into new creatures.

Abelard also denied Original Sin, and predestination, which puts him in the company of many of the heretics we have been studying recently. His method of teaching philosophy is attested to by a textbook he compiled, titled *Sic et Non*, "Yes and No," in which he raises a series of theological delimmas, and lists quotations from the writings of the church fathers which contradict each other. These contradictions in the writings of the church's authorities provided the jumping-off point of his lectures, and *Sic et Non* remains a much-studied text even today.

But the book which got him into the most trouble was called *On the Trinity*, in which he sought to clarify the thorny issue of how three persons could be one God. His arguments were so subtle and complex that his enemies decided it was the perfect vehicle to use to accuse him of heresy. And so in 1121 he was brought to trial in the local ecclesiastical court. His enemies had a hard time making their case from his book, and in fact, when finally allowed to speak in his defense, Abelard opened his book to the offending passage and pointed out that not only was the passage not his own opinion, but he was in fact merely quoting St. Augustine, and wouldn't they like to condemn him as well?

Unfortunately for Abelard, his enemies were well connected politically, and his book was formally condemned. Abelard's heart broke as he watched his work publicly denounced and then burned.

But Abelard was not himself excommunicated, not yet at least. He was allowed to return to the monastery, and the school he founded continued to flourish, drawing students from all over Europe to the study of theology.

Abelard also continued to write. We know so much about his history and his extraordinarily high opinion of himself from his autobiography, titled *The History of My Calamities*, which is some fun indeed. The full text is available on the World Wide Web and is well worth reading. The letters that he exchanged with Heloise during their monastic lives also still survive and continue to enjoy a wide readership.

Abelard was one of the most successful heretics, reaching even the rank of bishop as abbot of his own monastery, but his luck in this regard did not hold, I'm afraid. St. Bernard of Clairvaux, who favored mysticism to philosophy, found his teachings to be subversive to the faith and brought him to trial in 1140, nearly twenty years after his first heresy trial. This time, his enemies were more successful. He was condemned, and when Abelard appealed to Rome, the pope upheld the condemnation and excommunicated him. And yet, despite his condemnation, Abelard found refuge with the gentle monks of Cluny. Shortly before his death in 1142, Abelard and Bernard were reconciled. When Heloise died, they once again shared a bed, even if it was in death. They were buried together, and they remain together to this very day in their tomb in a cemetery in Paris.

So was Abelard really a heretic? Well, he held some unique opinions, and he certainly thought for himself. But Abelard's real undoing was not his ideas, but his passion. He was passionate about everything in his life: philosophy, teaching, fame, monasticism, and most especially, Heloise. Is that heresy? No. Is it sin? It certainly wouldn't be today. Today we would say Abelard was a brilliant idealist, a type-A personality, a passionate lover, and an arrogant snit. These are not crimes. But he was not a product of our time. He knew only the middle ages, and the modernity of his thought would surely have been considered sin in his day. But his greatest misfortunes were not ultimately caused by his questionable morality, but by the sheer force of his brilliance and the envy it aroused in the hearts of those who were blessed neither with his talent for thinking creatively nor the courage to do so.

God of the body, God of the mind, your servant Abelard dared to sin boldy, to love boldly, and to think boldly. Grant us a measure of his courage and save us from his portion of misfortunes, even as we learn from his brilliance and his folly. For we ask this in the name of the one who was not afraid to live human life to the fullest, and calls us to do the same, even Jesus Christ. Amen.

⊕ *Preached at Grace North Church August 27, 2000.*

13 | Peter Waldo

When I was in high school, I studied avidly in order to be licensed to preach by my congregation, Berea Baptist Church in Woodridge, Illinois. Our class of "preacher-boys" was taught by our Pastor, Brother Frank, and even then it was clear to me that the class was long on dogma and short on homiletical skills. We practiced on each other, we practiced at the roller rink, we practiced at the nursing home. And finally, we were granted the boon of delivering the Sunday night sermon, a much-coveted slot for us preacher-boys.

One of the guys in my class was a good-natured Italian fellow named Frank (oddly, the majority of men in our congregation were named Frank—it's a Bermuda Triangle kind of thing). Frank was the brother-in-law of my first real girlfriend, Kathy. Now Kathy was a lanky lass with a great sense of humor and a funky fashion sense. Best of all for a sixteen-year-old like myself who was just starting to feel his hormones, she was an awesome kisser.

Frank, like the rest of Kathy's family, was kind of a trip. He laughed a lot, even if he wasn't terribly smart. For evidence of this, I present the fact that only twenty-four hours after he met Kathy's sister, they were married and had moved into her parents' basement. Even then I thought that sounded like an ill-conceived plan, even if it was sickeningly romantic. But Frank and his bride seemed blissfully happy in their basement home. Go figure.

Like the rest of Kathy's clan, Frank was raised Roman Catholic and found his spiritual liberation in the Baptist faith. No more would their lives be ruled by capricious priests. No more would they worry about purgatory or the certainty of their salvation. They were whole-hearted converts to the notion of the priesthood of the believer, and Frank was positively giddy to find a community where even he, a married, non-celibate man with barely a high school education and no formal theological training, could be licensed to the Gospel ministry, authorized to marry 'em, dunk 'em, and bury 'em, and best of all, stand up before the assembly and bring 'em the Word of God.

Finally the night came when Frank would be bringing us the sermon on Sunday night. I'm afraid I can remember none of the details. I only remember sliding down in my seat, cringing in embarrassment for the poor guy, thinking, "Oh my god, this is terrible." After all, at the ripe old age of sixteen I had sat through nearly 800 sermons in my short life, so hey, I had some idea of what went into making a good one. Frank's wasn't, but that didn't diminish his enthusiasm any. He beamed like the sun itself after the service, and everyone told him what a brilliant job he had done. Frank went on to deliver horribly inept sermons at every opportunity, overjoyed at finding a religion where even someone like him could stand up and make the Good News sound bad and still receive a storm of praise for it.

Frank would have felt right at home in the twelfth century movement begun by a layman like himself named Peter Waldo. Waldo was a wealthy merchant in Lyons, France. One day while he was hosting a lavish banquet at his mansion, one of his guests suddenly fell over dead. Not only did this bring a quick halt to the festivities, but it also arrested Waldo's conscience. Not long after, he was listening to a troubadour singing the tale of St. Alexis, who sold all he had and went on a pilgrimage to the Holy Land. The troubadour sung of Alexis' holy death in his father's house, and it struck Waldo at his very core.

The very next morning he high-tailed it to the school of theology and began asking questions, which, as you might expect, was not entirely welcome. Still, he found one patient soul to instruct him, and was taught the many paths that discipleship could take. Baffled by the choices presented to him, he asked his teacher which was the most *certain* way to salvation. His instructor told him, "If thou wilt be perfect, go and sell all that thou hast, and give to the poor, and thou shalt have treasure in heaven; and come and follow Me."

Waldo was obsessed by this advice, and according to a surviving account of Waldo's conversion, he signed all of his property over to his wife, and gave all of his cash to the poor. He began preaching to the masses, warning that people cannot serve two masters, God and money. He felt he had been liberated from the lies perpetuated by society when he surrendered his money, and he called on others to do likewise.

Of course, this meant he had to beg for his meals. His wife was so horrified by this that she hauled him by the ear before the archbishop of the city, and practically throttling him, made the case that no one should be allowed to give poor Waldo any alms but her, a request that the bishop—no doubt baffled by this outbreak of neurotic religiosity—granted.

Waldo's conversion was dramatic and sincere, and soon he had gathered around him quite a swarm of followers. Like my friend Frank, none of them were very educated, certainly not in matters of religion, and yet Waldo bid them to go forth in twos, just as Jesus had bid the disciples, carrying nothing but the clothes on their backs, and preach the gospel in every city they came to.

At first, the Pope was pleased by the zeal of what were then called "The Poor Men of Lyons," and their efforts gained a measure of official support. But this did not last long, because along with the support came a number of restrictions, all of which they ignored. Not only that, but they began attacking the corruption of the papacy and the hierarchical structure of the church in general—never a safe policy.

They eschewed marriage, and sent both men and women out to preach. In fact, everyone who followed Waldo preached. It was a movement made up entirely of missionaries, and everyone who felt compelled to follow the preaching of this charismatic layman left their home and wealth behind and set out on the road to preach the Gospel. They were so single-minded and dedicated that the Waldenses, as they came to be called, spread quickly throughout Europe.

The Waldenses felt that not only could ordinary Christians preach, but they could also absolve people from sin, say Masses, and perform any of the other sacraments they deemed necessary.

Not surprisingly, all of this caused a great deal of alarm to the church's authorities, who were at a bit of a loss as to how to deal with a sect that did not formally separate itself from the church, was widely diffused into the general population, and had no structure to speak of that they could attack. Some Waldenses splintered into more and more heretical and extreme sects, and some considered themselves a reform movement within the Catholic church itself. And since there was no governing body, what the Waldenses movement actually *was* depended largely upon which Waldenses you asked.

The hierarchy was running scared, and things began to get ugly for Waldo and his followers. Waldo appealed to the Third Lateran Council in 1179 to give a defense of his ideas, but the bishops refused to hear him. Five years later he was formally excommunicated for his heretical teachings. Of course, this did not slow the movement down any, and it gained not only an increasing number of missionary members, but greater acceptance by the general population, who had grown suspicious of rich and powerful clergy. According to church historian David Christie-Murray, the Waldenses were "blameless in their lives, being humble, industrious toilers with their hands, who dressed simply, were temperate in all their appetites, sober, truthful, slow to anger, eschewing the gathering of wealth, and avoiding taverns, dances, and similar worldly pleasures." The general population were in awe of them.

Finally, the Catholic officials felt that the best way to take the wind out of their sails was to form an officially sanctioned group within the church itself, in order to effectively sort out the wheat from the chaff. Thus, in 1208, Pope Innocent III formed what he called "The Poor Catholics" which supported those parts of Waldo's movement the church could tolerate, while keeping a short leash on its members. It was a brilliant "if you can't beat 'em, join 'em" kind of move, one the church would employ again successfully hundreds of years later when battling the supposed "Masonic menace" by forming the Knights of Columbus as a rival fraternal organization for faithful Catholics.

In retrospect, the Catholic authorities were amazingly tolerant of the Waldenses at first. They tried persuasion whenever they could, and only resorted to force when peaceful avenues had been exhausted. The first group of them were burned at the stake as early as 1212, and they soon became the target of the inquisition. Oppression, of course, only strengthened their resolve and zeal for the true faith, and one fateful day in 1393, 150 were burned *en masse*.

Those that remained free fled to the Italian Alps, but even there they were not safe, as Pope Innocent VIII organized an entire crusade against them alone, and their numbers were decimated.

But they were not wiped out or discouraged from what they felt was the "true faith." Was this faith heretical? Well, today, we probably wouldn't call them heretics, but Protestants. One could make a good case that it was in fact Peter Waldo, not Martin Luther, that kicked off the Reformation. For it was Waldo who instituted the doctrine of the "priesthood of the believer" in deed if not in name, and nearly all of his reforms were shared by the later Reformers.

The Waldenses, against all odds, survived every assault Rome hurled at them. The crusaders were not able to root them all out, and when Calvin organized his reforms in Geneva, the Waldenses recognized the faith of the Reformed Christians as nearly identical to their own, and the remaining Waldenses were absorbed into the Swiss reformation.

So what can we learn from Peter Waldo and his followers? Waldo showed us that in his own age, as in any other, not everyone is willing to blindly follow when someone tries to pull the wool over their eyes. It was common sense to Waldo that the religious system of his day was corrupt, and that in his earnest desire to follow Christ, he could tolerate no compromise.

We also see that once again, the Holy Spirit will not be confined or controlled by any human institution. As Gerard Manly Hopkins would write nearly a thousand years later, "the Grandeur of God will flame out like shining from shook foil." God is not a tame lion, will not obey arbitrary human rules, and those who are in touch with the Spirit within them likewise cannot be controlled. Waldo and those who followed him were proto-Protestants, whose singular devotion to the lifestyle and teachings of Christ drove them into opposition with the establishment. And like Martin Luther, John Calvin, and even Martin Luther King after him, his devotion presaged the conflict that *must* follow when people of true faith try to live the Gospel with integrity.

For the Gospel does not support society, or the *status quo*, as so many preachers and priests who owe their livelihoods to "the system" would have us believe. The human spirit, like the Spirit of God, is indomitable in its quest for freedom, for salvation, and for the right to preach the Gospel, whether you are clergy or lay, an eloquent orator, or like my friend Frank, a dreadful preacher. God wants to use us all, and Frank, God bless him, like Peter Waldo before him, was simply willing. May God grant all of us such courage and willingness to be a minister no matter what station of life we are called to, no matter what our talents or lack of same, no matter who we are or what we have done. All Christians are priests, and have a responsibility to share the Good News with the little bit of the world that is ours. Let us go forth into the world and proclaim the good news of God's grace and good will to every creature.

God of the high and low alike, you are no respecter of persons, and you have instilled in all of us a calling to be the bearer of grace and good tidings to the world. Help us to have the courage of your servant Peter Waldo, the willingness to abandon those things which impair our spiritual progress, and the guts to confront corruption and evil wherever we find it. For though the cost may be great, we ignore such things at the peril of our souls and the souls of those who come after us. Teach us, O God, to hear your Spirit, even when it whispers things that are hard for us to hear, for we ask this in the name of the one who followed you, even unto death, Jesus Christ, your beloved child. Amen.

⊕ *Preached at Grace North Church September 24, 2000.*

14 | Mani & His Progeny

Near the beginning of this series on heresy I gave a sermon on Gnosticism, one of my favorite heresies. Gnosticism, as you may recall, turns the garden of Eden story on its ear. God is the bad guy, the snake is the good guy, and the souls of human beings are sparks of light trapped in a kingdom of darkness. We reincarnate in this insufferable veil of tears until we gain the knowledge of our true plight—*gnosis*—and are released into the embrace of the true godhead.

Christian gnosticism was forcefully stamped out in the third century, and though it no longer posed an imminent problem to the church, shreds of Gnostic teaching were popping up everywhere, mixing with all kinds of religious systems.

One of these strange syncretic religions was begun by a brilliant prophet and theologian named Mani. Mani was from Persia, and took Zoroastrianism as his starting point. In Zoroastrianism, there are two coeternal powers, good and evil. The universe is engaged in a cosmic battle between these two forces, and although the powers of good are assured victory, it is not going to be a pretty fight.

The prophet Zoroaster was hugely successful, and there are practicing Zoroastrians today. But the orthodox Zoroastrians did not take kindly to Mani's speculative cosmology, and he was exiled to India, where he picked up even more ideas, chiefly from Buddhism.

Finally, he returned to his native land, but by this time he had constructed an impressive theology that borrowed freely from Zoroastrianism, Christianity, Judaism, and Buddhism. Mani declared that there were four great prophets; not surprisingly, they were Zoroaster, Buddha, Jesus, and himself.

One problem with trying to encapsulate Mani's system is that it is hopelessly complex. Nevertheless, I shall try to give you a brief rundown of it here.

In the beginning, Mani taught, before the existence of heaven and earth, there were two separate natures, good and evil. These two natures were eternal and coexistent. The good nature was known as the Father of Greatness and lived in the place of Light. The evil principle was called the King of Darkness, and there was a great wall separating the two kingdoms.

The Kingdom of Darkness attacked the Kingdom of Light. But the Kingdom of Light was pacifistic and refused to fight back. Instead, the world of light created a savior, called Primal Man. Primal Man was defeated by the powers of Darkness, and his soul was taken hostage and imprisoned in corruption. When Primal Man regained his senses, he called out for help. In response, the Father of Greatness created a being called Living Spirit, who freed Primal Man. Unfortunately, his soul was still imprisoned. So Living Spirit tried a different tack. This time he created the cosmos, but not out of nothing. He created the universe out of the corpses of the powers of Darkness. The world then became a prison for the powers of Darkness, and very little light—the soul of the Primal Man—remained, where it strove to be purified from the corruption that housed it and return to the world of Light. So the Father of Greatness created some more; he made a Messenger, a new savior, and also plants and animals. Not to be outdone, the King of Darkness created bodies to trap and hold fast the soul of Primal Man. These bodies he called Adam and Eve.

The Father of Greatness sent Jesus, the new savior, into the world, who bid Adam eat of the Tree of Knowledge. Instantly his eyes were opened, and he saw Jesus as the personification of all Light trapped in darkness, the archetype of the eternal struggle of the light to be free of its fetters.

Like Adam, we too can eat of the Fruit by following the teachings of Mani, who held that it was possible for all beings in whom the spark of true light resides to be liberated and rejoin the Father of Greatness, even if it takes a thousand reincarnations to get there.

Now unlike earlier Gnostics, Mani was not interested in forming a small circle of esoteric elite. No, he wanted his religion to be universal, available to anyone, and very much out in the open. You can almost see them marching with banners that say, "We're here, we're dualists, get used to it!"

Not that Mani's system was totally devoid of elitism. In the Manichean church, there were two classes of people: the hearers and the elect. Now if you were a member of the elect, you abstained from all sexual practices and were a strict vegetarian, but when you died, you went straight to the world of Light. But if you were a hearer you could have a family, eat pretty much what you wanted, but unfortunately, you would continue to reincarnate until you mustered the intestinal fortitude to live as one of the elect.

Not everyone was terribly pleased by Mani's efforts and in the year 275 he was crucified by Persian emperor Bahram I. But like all good martyrs, Mani's death just spurred his followers onwards all the more, and they launched missionary efforts that literally spanned the known world.

One of the most famous Manichees was St. Augustine, who lived as a Manichee hearer for eleven years before he converted to Christianity. But many scholars question just how far this conversion went, as Augustine took many Manichean teachings, such as the corrupt nature of matter and the great evil of sexuality, and through powerful friends and a great sphere of influence, made such abysmal teachings the dogma of the Christian church.

Although Manichean missionaries went far abroad, his influence in his native Persia eventually waned, and his followers were absorbed by the native Zoroastrianism.

Flash forward nearly five hundred years, to what is now known as Bulgaria. The ruler of Bulgaria at that time was Khan Boris I, who was having difficulty holding his kingdom together. His people espoused a variety of paganisms, and he was perceived by the rest of the world to be kind of a two-bit monarch. Eager to change this perception, Boris was sure that converting to Christianity would provide the stability and respectability that his kingdom lacked. So he was baptized, and declared Bulgaria a Christian nation. The Orthodox church moved in and started taking over.

One of the methods the Orthodox church used to keep uncooperative elements (read "religious dissenters") under control was to forcibly relocate them in a more Christian area, where the local piety was sure to rub off on the pesky dissidents.

Thus in the year 872, the Orthodox church dumped a load of uncooperative Manicheans on the Bulgarian frontier.

Far from converting the Manicheans, quite the opposite happened. The newcomers introduced their faith to the fledgling Christians in Bulgaria, who found their version of events endlessly more entertaining, and by the year 950, a new sect called the Bogomils was born.

The Bogomils didn't receive Mani's revelation whole, but large parts of it remained intact, and it is considered by most scholars to be the continuation of the Manichean tradition.

One of the differences was that the Father of Darkness was known as Satanael, who was God's first born son. Satanael out of pride set up his own empire with a following of angels. He was cast out of heaven for this, and so he made a new heaven and earth. Satanael also made human beings, but could not create the soul that would give humans life. So Satanael made a deal with his father: he would give humankind souls only if the souls that Satanael had taken from heaven were replaced with souls from humankind. Satanael agreed, and the deal was done. But then Satanael reneged on the deal and sought to keep humankind enslaved forever. He set himself up as god, called himself Yahweh, and made the Jews worship him.

God's second-born son and Satanael's brother was Jesus, as you might have guessed. Jesus came to earth to overthrow his brother's evil empire. Satanael tried to kill him, but Jesus tricked him. His body wasn't real, but just an illusion, and so no harm was done to him at the crucifixion. Jesus returned to heaven and took over Satanael's seat of power there.

This sounds different from Mani's myth, but really, only the names have changed. We still have the powers of good battling the powers of evil. Humankind is, in both systems, trapped in matter and longs to return to the godhead. And Jesus is still the messenger of Light who shows humanity the way to be free.

Bogomilism gained a lot of popularity, partly because it provided a much more credible answer to the problem of evil than did Christianity.

If God was all good, and the world is good, and if God is all-powerful, why is there so much evil and suffering in the world? If God is all-powerful, would he not simply destroy evil? If God was all good, why would he suffer evil to exist?

The Christian church has never provided credible answers to these questions, but the Bogomils had a great answer. The world is in such a mess because it is the handiwork of an evil being, intent upon our bondage and continued miring in corruption. And since the evil powers that created the world were seen as the worldly authorities from which the political authorities derived their power, Bogomils were far from model citizens.

As one Orthodox priest wrote of them at the time, "They teach their adherents not to submit to the authorities, they denigrate the rich, they hate the emperors, they rail at superiors, they insult the lords, they hold that God abhors those who work for the emperor, and they urge every servant not to labor for his master."

Like their Manichean forbears, Bogomils believed the world was evil, and that one should avoid contact with it at all costs. Thus they abstained from sex, the eating of meat, and the drinking of wine. At the same time, they accused the Orthodox clergy of idleness, drunkenness, and robbery, which was no doubt true, at least in part.

People perceived the Bogomils as being much more authentic and credible in their faith than the Orthodox, and their numbers grew. They met little resistance for about a hundred years, when they started sending missionaries out into the wider Byzantine empire.

The emperor and the church officials felt that this would simply not do, and they devised a plan to put an end to the Bogomil threat. In the early twelfth century, the emperor called Basil, the leader of the Bogomils at that time, to the palace. The emperor told him he was interested in converting, and wanted to hear the Bogomils' teaching from the horse's mouth, as it were. All during the interview, a scribe was hidden behind a curtain, taking down furious notes on everything Basil said. After the interview, Basil was arrested, and all of his followers who could be found were imprisoned with him.

Basil and his followers were told that they would be burned alive unless they recanted and became Orthodox Christians. They refused. Thus in 1119, a huge pyre was built at the Hippodrome in Constantinople. Basil was given the choice of walking to the pyre to be burned, or walking to a cross, where he would be baptized and set free. Not surprisingly, Basil held fast to his faith and chose the pyre.

The crowd cheered and demanded the same choice for the other Bogomils, but the emperor refused, and the other Bogomils spent the rest of their lives in prison, where, ancient authorities tell us, they were well-treated and supplied with adequate food and clothing.

Those Bogomils who escaped continued to practice their faith, and they even gained a certain degree of imperial favor in centuries to come. Finally, when the Turks subjugated the Balkans and overthrew the Orthodox rulers, the people were given another chance to convert, but this time to Islam. Many of the Bogomils, who by this time were fed up with being mistreated by Christians, took them up on the offer, and the Bogomils were absorbed into Islam.

But the story does not end there! For there were numerous missionary journeys undertaken by the Bogomils, some of them in the West. Unfortunately, the Bogomils did not fare so well in the West as they did in the East.

The missionaries to the West founded a church of followers called the "cathari" or "the pure ones." We call them the Cathars today. Based in their stronghold in southern France, they had thriving centers in Italy, Yugoslavia, Switzerland, and Germany.

The teachings of the Cathars were virtually identical to the Bogomils, and their appeal to the general populace was similar as well. Roman Catholic clergy were just as corrupt and lazy as the Orthodox clergy, and the common folk were attracted to the Cathars' piety.

The Cathars did not honor rituals such as marriage, baptism, or communion, but they did develop an odd rite called the "Consolamentum" which was bestowed upon the "elect" or inner circle and freed him or her from the power of Satan, and guaranteed the follower that he or she would escape this world upon death.

The Cathars were converting huge numbers, especially in southern France. This was an intolerable situation for the Roman Catholic church, of course, and the Cathars caught wind of trouble brewing. Many nobles in that area were Cathars, and so in 1204, they began to fortify one of their strongholds, Montsegur, and to ready it for battle. There is a legend that the Cathars were the keepers of the Holy Grail, which was enshrined at Montsegur. In 1209 an entire crusade was launched against this lowly tribe of latter-day Manicheans, the first crusade directed at fellow Christians, even if those Christians *were* heretics. A madman named Simon de Montfort led the charge, and whole villages of Cathari were brutally massacred. When asked how the crusaders would be able to tell the Cathars from the Catholics, the papal legate Arnaud sneered, "Kill them all. God will know his own."

The Cathars were determined, however, and their castle at Montsegur withstood the crusaders' attacks. In 1215 the Inquisition was founded, and the crusaders renewed their charge.

After six months of brave defense, Montsegur finally fell to the crusaders through an act of treachery, and in March 1244, the Cathars were captured.

205 Cathari were led down the mountain, singing hymns with their heads held high. They marched straight into the bonfires built for them and perished. Whatever remnant of the Cathari that were left either went East to the Balkans, or, like the Manicheans and the Bogomils before them, they were absorbed into the dominant religion of the area, in this case, Catholic Christianity.

There are many people who believe that the secret teachings of the Cathars were shared by the Knights Templar, who, when they fell in the late middle ages, escaped to Scotland, where they founded the Scottish Rite Masons, an organization in which the secret teachings of Mani survive even to this day.

What a story! What a legacy! And what craziness! So what lessons can we learn from the Manichees and their progeny; what gifts do they bring to us?

One lesson is clear: faith must be credible in order to flourish. The Bogomils and Cathari alike flourished precisely because of this factor. The Christians did not have an acceptable answer to the problem of evil, a problem which the Manichean theology solved handily. But they were also credible in that they lived their faith in a way that was convincing to their neighbors. They were in every way morally superior to the authorities of the established churches. They were tireless in works of mercy, chaste in their sexual lives, and strict in their observances. Their faith was convincing, both in its theology and in its practice.

This is something we are desperately in need of today. Though Mani's cosmology sounds hopelessly complicated when you really get into it, to the intelligentsia of his day it had a ring of scientific authority which was convincing. In our own time, many are quick to dismiss Christianity as being irrelevant, an outdated mythology with no real connection to our daily lives.

If one takes mythology literally, they are quite right. The buffoonery of the televangelists betrays the intellectual ineptitude of fundamentalist Christianity. And don't talk to me about piety. Self-righteousness is not the same as righteousness, as even a casual observer of Jimmy Swaggart's fall can see.

So is Christianity morally and theologically bankrupt? Hardly. Every mythology worth its salt must reinvent itself in every generation. We may use the same symbols as Christians down through the ages, but we also often mean vastly different things by them. For ancient Christians, for example, the Eucharist recalled for them the table-fellowship Jesus shared with them; for later Christians it became the symbol of the transformation of the universe; still later it became a reenactment of the crucifixion; and in our own day, the Eucharist is seen as a foretaste of the great feast at the end of the world, where all peoples will be seated at God's table, the lion will lie down with the lamb, and the reign of universal peace and prosperity begins.

Symbols might remain the same, but in order to remain efficacious, they must also retain their plasticity.

In the Manicheans, the Bogomils, and the Cathari, the ancient teachings of the Gnostics found new wineskins, providing hope for countless people of faith. This is the path of all faithful people—not Gnosticism, of course, but the reinvention of tradition. God grant us a measure of the creativity, earnestness, and true faith of these ancient heretics, and hopefully, a happier end.

Father of Greatness, you who dwell in ineffable light, visit upon us the creativity and zeal of these ancient people of faith; not that we may supplant the dominant religion, but so that our faith may be likewise heartfelt and alive. For we ask this in the name of the one who came into this world of seeming darkness for our salvation, even Jesus Christ. Amen.

⊕ *Preached at Grace North Church October 22, 2000.*

15 | Meister Eckhart

Today, when I visit my parents and attend church with them, they are as likely to criticize the pastor as to praise his sermon on the ride home. But this would never have occurred when I was a child. I never heard my parents disparage the preacher, and if they ever did, they did it out of earshot of me. Maybe we just had better preachers back then, but my guess is that my parents were just starstruck and gullible when they were young adults, and have grown more cynical and jaded about the church since then. Good for them, I say, because in retrospect everyone I knew held the preacher in way too much esteem in those days, certainly more than any mortal man deserves. For in my young, impressionable eyes back then, the preacher was the top of the pyramid. Out of anyone else in the church, he was sprinting ahead towards the kingdom of light, while the rest of us hobbled along behind. If anyone had "made it" in the spiritual world, he had. If anyone was pure, he was; and if anyone was omniscient, well, he was the closest. The idolization of clergy by evangelicals is kind of a mystery, since they are just as likely as anyone else to suffer moral breakdowns, but I got the message, loud and clear. The preacher had *made it*. God approved of him, and tolerated the rest of us due to his superior holiness. Like Moses lifting high the bronze serpent in the wilderness, the preacher was all that stood between us and God's most deserved wrath.

One irony in all of this is that, as much as evangelicals eschew anything even remotely Catholic, the evangelical and puritanical model of holiness is startlingly similar to the hierarchical model of holiness found in the Catholic Church.

This hierarchy is reflected upon with greater consciousness in Catholic thought, of course. Catholics have long applied Aristotelian categorization and intense intellectual reflection to this subject, while evangelicals tend to content themselves with a vague doctrine of "sanctification." In the well-defined medieval schema, however, we find little that any modern evangelical would disagree with.

In the medieval model of holiness, we see a ladder with three rungs. The first rung to be achieved by the person striving for holiness was "purgation," or the emptying of oneself of all sin, all desire, all selfish motivations, empty of all save for the thirst for God. This step happened at humankind's instigation. The next step was up to God. This step is called "illumination," where divine inspiration is visited upon a person—though it was usually only monks who had the leisure for this type of intensive spiritual practice. This illumination is similar to the Gnostic visitation of "gnosis" or divine knowledge upon a person, and not dissimilar to many charismatic evangelicals' ecstatic experiences of the Holy Spirit. The final rung of this ladder was "union," where the aspirant, having been both emptied of the world, and then filled by the spirit, achieves a state of oneness with God. Now this ladder only allows for one-way traffic. You can only go up, and you only need do it once. After reaching the blessed state of "union," you've "made it," big time.

I always wanted to "make it" as far as God is concerned when I was a kid. If I had known about the three-step ladder of purgation, illumination, and union, I would have started stepping in grade school. So perhaps it is fortunate we were not Catholics. It was enough to simply idolize the preacher. After all, if anyone had "made it," it was him.

If I am honest with myself, I have to admit that one of my unconscious motivations in being called to the priesthood was this desire to "make it" in God's eyes. I have always had this nagging suspicion that I was damned (probably the result of being a very creative person in a very stifling tradition that could not accommodate my creative thinking), and, irrationally, I suppose, a part of me thought that if I were ordained, I would be good enough, that God would take notice of me, forgive and accept me, that I would finally be a "made man," as Tony Soprano might say.

It will come as no surprise to you that it did not happen that way. I lay prostrate before the bishop, felt him smear the oil on my forehead, put his hands on my head, and said my first mass. And wouldn't you know? Afterwards, I was the same insecure and neurotic schmuck I was before I began.

It was a hard lesson. After I got over it, however, and got on with the actual daily grind of priesting, I discovered that holiness is not an ascent, it is not a one-way climb up a ladder, it is not a grace visited once and for all upon a person. Instead, the spiritual life is a journey that never ends, never reaches the summit, at least in this life, and that there are no "made men," even if you are the Pope or the Dalai Lama.

Meister Eckhart, a German clergyman who lived and wrote in the fourteenth century, knew this hard truth well. We don't know many details about Meister Eckhart's early life. He was probably born just before 1260 in a little village called Hochheim. Like me, his given name was probably John, and he entered the Dominican order as a very young man. He studied theology at Cologne and Paris, earning his master's degree, and thus his nickname "Meister," around 1294. But in 1300 he was sent back to Germany to begin his ministry proper. He must have done well in his post as Vicar of Thuringia, because three years later he was appointed the Provincial of the entire Dominican Order in one sizable province which contained upwards of sixty religious communities.

Eckhart was successful not only with the hierarchy, but with the common folks as well, for unlike most clergymen, he felt that the spirituality of the common folk was important, and angered many of his contemporaries by preaching and writing prolifically in common German, which was tantamount to heresy in his time.

But when challenged, he simply said, "If the ignorant are not taught they will never learn; the business of the doctor is to heal," and the people loved him for this. He taught them not only in their own tongue, but using images and examples that they could readily understand. He was also very supportive of alternative religious communities such as the Beguines, who were not exactly nuns, but not laywomen either. Beguines were more like religious communes for women who simply loved God. These communities made the church and society very nervous, as these pesky and upstart women were not married, so had no husbands to keep them in line, but nor were they under the authority of the church, and it simply would not do to have a woman who could make up her own mind about anything—heaven forbid! But Eckhart supported and offered guidance to the Beguines and other non-traditional communities, and his fame grew.

But it was not simply his style and approach to ministry that made him so beloved, it was also *what* he taught that was so extraordinary. For Eckhart was not a pedant, but a mystic.

In his view, the idea that there was any distinction between God and the material world was an illusion, and a dangerous one at that. God and humankind were made of the same stuff, Eckhart said, and shared one being. He is known to have said that "the eye with which I see God is the same eye with which God sees me." For Eckhart, there is no distinction between God and human, between creator and creation, and scraping the scales off of people's eyes so that they could behold this awesome truth was his life's work.

One amazing implication of this theology, of course, is that no one needs to strive to achieve union with God; it is already a given. One does not have to work for it, one has only to enjoy it. No one needs to "make it" in God's eyes, and in Eckhart's world there were no "made men," since all creation is already "made."

So if spiritual growth for Eckhart was not a ladder to the sky, how did it happen? Surely people grow, surely their apprehension of spiritual reality must mature, but if not hierarchically, then how?

Eckhart's answer was "cyclically." Eckhart wrote of the "four paths" of spiritual growth that everyone participates in, whether they know it or not. The key is to participate in it consciously, to follow the flow of the paths as they merge one into the other, and to be aware as one's spiritual life takes root and deepens.

The first path Eckhart called the "Via Positiva" or the way of wonder. The first step in the spiritual life is awe, gratitude, and amazement. One brilliant sunset is enough to kick it off, just as the close examination of a dog's paw can inspire similar wonder, or even the ecstasy found in the arms of one's beloved. All are occasions for awe. Wonder is all around us; for the goodness God proclaimed in the Creation of the world has not been diminished by human sin, but only made more poignantly apparent.

But just as one cannot climb a mountain without coming down, the first path inevitably gives way to the second, the "Via Negativa," the way of sinking, cooling, of darkness, pain, and letting go. The second path is harder than the first, for it teaches us that all those things that cause such feelings of awe and wonder in us must all come to an end. All things rise and fall. Joy is followed by sorrow, light is followed by darkness, ecstasy is followed by agony. But Eckhart insists this is not a bad thing at all, but a necessary and holy thing. God does not wish us to live in an illusion that everything is sweetness and light, for pain and loss are also our teachers and also very real. Instead of insulating ourselves from pain, Eckhart insists that we embrace the Negativa, to enter it willingly and with courage, knowing that it is not the last step, pain is not the end of our journey. But the dark valley must be gone through before the next rise can be approached. We must learn the lessons of the valley before the next path is possible. The Negativa has many gifts to impart: detachment, not taking ourselves too seriously, and the ability to let go and let God, as the saying goes. Letting go and letting be is the hardest part of the spiritual journey, but without it our travels are aborted. If we can walk through the valley, a great prize awaits us: the Via Creativa—the way of creativity—the next stage in our journey. Once we have emptied ourselves in the Negativa, we are ready to be filled. The Creativa is the result, as our pain provides the fuel for our creative expression. As we give form to our experience, our experience is transformed. In the act of creativity, God speaks with our mouth, draws with our pen, sings with our voice. The wonder and pain of all of creation pours through us as the spirit of God in us gives us utterance. Art, music, poetry, dance, cooking, woodworking, even sermon-writing are ways in which sense is made of the first two paths, and God is made flesh once again.

The Via Creativa, the proclamation in art of both our joy and our sorrow, cannot help but have an effect on us and others as well. For as we share these experiences, as our art is heard and understood, even by ourselves, we are already embarking on the fourth and final path: the Via Transformativa, the way of transformation and reformation. In this path, we are moved by the art we produce to act in the world, to make it better, to elevate suffering, to encourage the downtrodden, to feed the hungry and visit the sick, to challenge the powerful on behalf of the weak. The Transformativa is what the Jews call *"Tikkun,"* the remaking of the world, in which God is just as dependent upon us as we are upon God.

These then are the four paths of spiritual growth: the Via Positiva, the Via Negativa, the Via Creativa, and the Via Transformativa. Wonder ushers us into sorrow, wonder and sorrow together move us to express our inmost being, and this expression moves us and others toward social justice and communal transformation.

Wonderful, isn't it? But the most amazing thing about this model of spiritual growth is that it is not hierarchical. No one "makes it," because as soon as you have finished with the Via Transformativa, a child's smile will catch your eye, the Via Positiva kicks in and the whole cycle starts all over again. Instead of a ladder to the sky, the four paths are a spiral that does not go up to the sky, but deepens until one is more and more grounded in the good earth, able to behold God in the most humble of creatures, able to cry with God at the seemingly most insignificant sorrows, able to express this tension to others, and able to move hearts—one's own as well as others—to make the world a place where God's face is more easily seen everywhere.

Everyone, whether they are aware of it or not, is always working one of the paths. The advantage to making this process conscious is that one is less likely to get stuck in one of them, especially the Negativa. And one is also more able to support others on their paths, as it is often evident which stage they are in, and one always knows what is coming next, and so in which direction they should head.

This non-hierarchical model of spiritual growth, as you might guess, did not sit well with the church hierarchy, for in 1325 a complaint against his teaching was brought before the Holy Inquisition. Eckhart delivered his protest to the Inquisition in 1327, and even offered a Declaration of Orthodoxy. His Declaration was, unfortunately, rejected.

But Eckhart had one more trick up his sleeve: good timing. Before his excommunication was handed down in 1329, he had the good sense to die while he was still in the good graces of the church. So, like Origen, that other great scholar and heretic before him, he died in safety, in the arms of Mother church, with the full benefits of last rights and Christian burial. By the time his excommunication was made official, Eckhart was already safely within the pearly gates, having the last laugh.

Eckhart has much to teach us. His theology has much in common with Buddhism, Taoism, and other unitive philosophies and religions, and many in these traditions claim him as one of their own. I don't think Eckhart would have minded. After all, in his view, it didn't matter what name one used to refer to God, for God only has one face: ours.

Holy Oneness, we stand before you in wonder, you sit beside us as we weep, you move through us as we shout our songs to the heavens, and you work in us as we labor to love our neighbor. Help us to see ourselves not as failures who can never scale the heights that holy people do, nor as people who have "made it" and no longer need to strive for perfection; but simply as your children, holy only because we are. Help us to notice all the joy and sorrow in this kaleidoscope world, to recognize you in it, and in ourselves, and give us strength and will to remake the world in your image. Amen.

⊕ *Preached at Grace North Church June 24, 2001.*

16 | Julian of Norwich

Have you ever had a vision? Ever been visited by an angel like Mary, or heard the voice of God like Joan of Arc? They're not that unusual, you know, but lots of folks are afraid to talk about them, especially since they tend to occur in times of great stress and emotional turmoil. People are afraid that folks will think they are crazy, or they discount their visions as psychotic episodes.

Of course, they are probably right about that. Most visionaries and many great artists are hopelessly mentally ill. But that does not discount the validity of the vision. The veil between the conscious world and the unconscious is thinner for people in distress or suffering from mental illness. Archetypal energies can leap forth into consciousness with greater ease in these cases—but when judging these people, we must remember that it is the same collective unconscious leaping out whether the recipient is crazy or sane. And truthfully, who among us has never felt a little crazy?

I certainly have. I remember when I was in college, I used to wake up in the middle of the night screaming and sweating from dreams of hellfire. Images of the monster God were leaping out at me from my literature studies. Eventually, I cried out to God in pain one night, "I cannot worship a monster. If you are a sadist, you cannot be my God, for I cannot serve the God of my parents. If there is something else out there, please show me." Because in truth, the

God I was raised with was more demonic than divine.

The true God answered this prayer. Twenty-four hours later a friend of mine suggested we visit St. Michael's Episcopal Church. "Let's see what C.S. Lewis and Charles Williams meant by church," he said. And so we went.

And I have never been the same. I was dumbstruck by the life-sized gory crucifix hanging halfway through the sanctuary from the rafters. The ritual spoke to something primal and wordless in me, and when communion was offered, I raced for the rail like a man dying of thirst in the desert coming upon an oasis. But it was when the communion wafer was placed on my tongue that it happened.

As soon as the bread hit my tongue, I felt a rushing wind wash over me, and I heard an audible voice whisper in my ear, "This is my mercy for you. Feel it on your tongue, taste it. It is real."

Weeping, I stumbled back to my place in the pew and wondered over what I had experienced.

It is the only time I have ever heard God's voice. It may very well be the last. One thing I know: it changed my life forever.

And while it propelled me on a renewed spiritual journey that has eventually led me here, it was also a damnedly troublesome experience for an agnostic. It is difficult to be an agnostic when God has spoken to you. Call it stubbornness, I suppose, but I give it a good shot!

I wasn't looking for a vision; it just happened to me, perhaps when I needed it most. But today's mystic, Julian of Norwich, wanted to have one desperately.

As a young woman, she prayed for a threefold favor from God: First she wanted to behold the crucifixion, to be as one who stood at the foot of the cross so that she might better comprehend Jesus' suffering, and share his compassion for the world. The second favor she asked was to be made deathly ill before she was thirty years old so that she might be purged of herself and be able to live more fully in the life of Christ. The third petition was that God would grant her three wounds: the wound of compassion, the wound of contrition, and the wound of willful longing toward God.

Perhaps it is not too surprising to us today, who are conscious of the fact that prophecies are often self-fulfilling, but her request was granted.

At the end of her twenty-ninth year she fell ill with an unspecified disease that brought her to the very brink of death. She herself believed that she was dying, and so did those around her. A priest was summoned who suspended a crucifix above her head and gave her the last rites.

And as she lay there, staring at the face of the crucifix, shuddering with fever, the crucifix came to life, and Julian was granted sixteen "shewings" or visions.

We know about these visions because soon after she recovered Julian wrote them down. Then, twenty years later, she wrote them down again, only this time with the benefit of twenty years of reflection. Thus we have a short manuscript and a longer manuscript from Julian. Both are valuable, but it is generally the longer version that is read popularly.

I highly recommend everyone in the congregation to hop down to Barnes and Noble and pick up a copy. It is widely available, and should be read by everyone on a spiritual path. Julian writes in Middle English, since she lived in the 14th century, and together with Geoffrey Chaucer, is one of early English's literary pioneers. In fact, hers is the first book written in English by a woman. Even though she calls herself "unlettered," this self-deprecation is transparent as soon as one begins reading. She is, in fact, a literary, political, and religious genius. And as one of the first women writers to be widely read, feminists like myself have much to rejoice at in her, not only for her literary achievements but also for her theological chutzpah.

Who was this amazing woman? No one knows. Her real name is lost to us. We call her Julian only because she was an anchoress at the church of St. Julian in Norwich, England. What is an anchoress, you might be asking, and the answer may shock you. An anchorite, or anchoress if she was a woman, was a person who allowed him or herself to be shut into a single room for the rest of his or her life. The church has since condemned what it calls "morbid seclusion" but in medieval times, it was actually quite common. Julian did not have a lonely life, however. One side of her room had a window into the church, so she could participate in the mass. Another window allowed her to commune with nature, receive her meals, and offer spiritual direction to the many pilgrims that came to her for advice. She also had the company of her beloved cat, and Julian is sometimes shown with her cat in icons. Soon after her illness, she requested to be shut up in the church of St. Julian, to better devote her life to prayer and meditation upon her visions, a request that was granted when she was installed on May 16, 1373.

Visions are a dime a dozen in the history of religions, and the church has always been suspicious of them. And yet Julian's visions were immediately recognized as being genuine, although it is true that not everyone appreciated what she had to say, as some of what she was shown was shocking indeed in her day, and may very well be shocking to some in ours.

It is difficult to pin down one main teaching to which she frequently returns, but several threads are discernable.

One of the most amazing revelations concerns God's wrath. She writes, "Holy Church taught me that sinners are sometimes worthy of blame and wrath, but I could not see these in God in my vision. [Instead,] I saw that our Lord was never wrathful, nor ever shall be...God is the goodness that cannot be wrathful."

I want you to notice what she is doing here. Julian is an obedient daughter of the church. Her self-image is that she is wholly and completely orthodox, not wanting to err in any way, nor in any way contradict church teaching. But she is in a quandary: her project is to relate what she saw of God in her visions, and the difficulty for her is that very often the things she saw do not jive with the teachings of the church. Julian has to peddle pretty hard sometimes to have it both ways.

In the excerpt I just read, she says, "Holy Church taught me that sinners are worthy of wrath," but then she has to admit the truth that she did not behold any wrath in God when she had her vision. The God Julian beheld on her sickbed was a God filled only with goodness. That which separates us from God is not God's wrath, or his offended honor, or God's need for justice, but simply our own shame, which God pleads with us to let go of so that we can enjoy communion with him.

This is in marked contrast to the theologians of Julian's day (who placed the block to communion between God and humanity in God); but Julian contradicts this, and says that God embraces us always, it is we who hide our faces from him. Not because God holds our sin against us, but because we live in shame of our sin and cannot let go of it. It is not that God will not forgive us, it is that we cannot forgive ourselves.

Julian says that in every person there is a part of them that does not consent to sin, and never will, and that is our true soul, which is at one with God, and ever shall be. Julian writes, "My own sin will not hinder the working of God's goodness. As long as we are in this life and find ourselves foolishly dwelling on sinfulness, our God tenderly touches us and joyfully calls us saying: 'Let all your love be, my child. Turn to me. I am everything you need. Enjoy me and your liberation.'"

Likewise, Julian tap dances deftly around the subject of Hell. She says that in her vision, "I had a desire to see Hell and Purgatory— not to have proof that they exist but rather to learn everything I had been taught in my faith so that my life might profit from this experience. But for all my desire, I did not see them."

See, she doesn't come right out and say, "There is no hell." Instead, she says, "The Holy Church teaches there is a hell, and so of course, it must be so; but *I did not see it.*" Thus, she cleverly protects her orthodoxy and challenges it in the very same statement.

But for all of her boldness, Julian's writings are most rewarding because of her deep mysticism. She invents many words in her book, no doubt because she had need of them and they did not yet exist. One word she uses over and over is "oneing." God "ones" us to himself, God is "oneing" the universe. Today we may say "uniting" or "atonement" but these have different shades of meaning. For Julian, as for Meister Eckhart, all the universe resides in God. "See!" she writes, "I am God. See! I am in everything. See! I do everything. See! I never lift my hands off my works, nor will I ever. See! I lead everything toward the purpose I ordained it to from without beginning. By the same Power, Wisdom, and Love by which I created it. How could anything be amiss?"

And this is the great comforting kernel of Julian's work: as distressing as sin, suffering, and evil is, as difficult as it is to reconcile these things to God's love, in the end Julian is convinced that "all things work together for the good," and in her visions she is told to be at peace. God is in control, God embraces the world in love always, and nothing and no one will ever be lost. "For all shall be well," she is told. "All shall be well, and every manner of thing shall be well."

This image of God the mother, cradling the world, cooing at it like a child, comforting it, and promising to keep it safe permeates

Julian's book. She calls Jesus "our mother in nature and in grace." The cross was his travail of childbirth, and we his children. The milk by which we are suckled is the sacraments, and the bosom to which we cling is his wounded side. We can run to him when we are hurting, and as Julian says, "The sweet gracious hands of our Mother will be ready and will be fast around us."

Julian is thus not only one of the first women ever to write in English, but she is most assuredly the first feminist theologian.

If we must have a single image with which to typify her visions, it would be her description of the hazelnut. She writes, "God showed me in my palm a little thing round as a ball, about the size of a hazelnut. I looked at it with the eye of my understanding and asked myself: 'What is this thing?' And I was answered: 'It is everything that is created.' I wondered how it could survive since it seemed so little it could suddenly disintegrate into nothing. The answer came, 'It endures and ever will endure, because God loves it.' And so everything has being because of God's love."

In Julian's vision she saw a God very different from the one she was given: instead of a God of wrath, she saw only of God of love; instead of Hell she saw only redemption; instead of sin she saw only illusion. Julian's God is big enough to hold the whole of the created universe in the palm of her hand, and yet nurses and supports it out of pure and eternal love. Yes, sin is troubling, she says, but all will be well. Yes, the church teaches God is wrathful and people go to Hell, but I could not see it. Yes, God is our father, but Jesus is our mother, he gave birth to us and he cradles us in love now and forever.

I'm not a very good agnostic, you know. I want to say, "I don't know if there is a God." Yet, like Julian, I have been visited, and the truth is, as much antipathy as I feel towards the God pushed by the church, I want to believe in the God of Julian with all my heart. And I think that, deep down, I do.

God of love and compassion, you hold us like a mother holds her child. You suckle us with spiritual food, and you test us but will not let us fall. Help us to let go of our shame, that we may let it drop away, and turn to face you with our hands empty, eager to embrace, and eagerly embraced. For we ask this in the name of the one who gave us birth, who sustains this earth our island home, and who whispers to her frightened children, "Shh, my love, for all shall be well, all shall be well, and every manner of thing shall be well." Amen.

⊕ *Preached at Grace North Church July 18, 2001.*

17 | Michael Servetus

One of the things I am going to miss the most about our friend Robert DeVelbiss (a highly-educated parishioner who died recently) is the constant challenge of preaching to him. It is a daunting task to preach to someone who clearly has twice as much book-learning as humans by rights *should* have; and it was an ever-present challenge to me to search and research my subjects until I happened upon that one nugget of obscure information that I wagered even Robert wouldn't know. I was not always successful, and it was rather like an academic competition every week. If at coffee hour after the service Robert nodded at me and said he enjoyed the sermon, I knew the match had gone to him, but if he wagged his cookie in my face and said, "I didn't know about such and such..." I knew the game had gone to me. Even though the odds were weighted heavily against me in every sermon, I am pleased to say that Robert and I in any given month usually pulled off a draw, a fact that I am very proud of indeed. It is a game which I will sorely miss.

This rooting around in the forgotten cellars of the church's history for arcane nuggets that shock and delight, those stories that knock your socks off, and yet which few in the congregation have ever heard before, are what make it all worth it for me. It was not only fun to preach for someone like Robert, but it also repeatedly challenged my own faith, and hopefully, it has surprised you a time or two as well.

One of the most monumental discoveries for me thus far occurred when I was researching my doctoral dissertation on the Holy Eucharist. In figuring out just how the Communion service expressed the church's hope for salvation down through the ages, I discovered that what the church actually taught about how we are saved has changed again and again, and with these changes, our understanding of the Eucharist shifted as well. I remember when I happened upon the Christus Victor theory of the atonement. In brief, it is the idea that we are not saved by the crucifixion at all, but by the resurrection. This theory teaches that the sin of Adam effected the devolution of the universe; all things were devolving into chaos. But when Christ rose from the dead, that devolution was halted, and the universe began to evolve into divinity itself, a process which is dependent on human beings for its fulfillment. This theory blew me away, for it is not focused upon punishment for sin, but instead on the divinity of all things. It does not glorify suffering as the teaching of the cross does, nor does it view creation as corrupt and irredeemable. It values human beings and the rest of creation as God's right arm in the process of salvation.

What a gift this discovery was to me! I felt liberated, vindicated that so many of my ideas about who God is and how humans relate to God were supported by this ancient teaching, which is still the dominant theology of the Eastern Orthodox Churches.

Theology can set you free! I truly don't understand why more people don't study it—for like great literature, it addresses everything we are as human beings. It challenges us, prods us, makes us angry, makes us think, makes us fight back, and sets us free. *Viva theology!*

I am not the only cheerleader the church has had for the liberating power of theology. Our mystic *de jour*, Michael Servetus, was likewise liberated by his studies, a liberation which, unfortunately, was not eagerly embraced by his time.

Servetus was born in 1511 in Spain, amidst the fevered pitch of the Inquisition's two-headed battle against the Protestants to the North and against those pesky Jews and Muslims in their midst and to the South.

Servetus was possessed of an intellect to rival even Robert's. His areas of expertise extended to jurisprudence, mathematics, meteorology, geography, astrology, philosophy, theology, and biblical criticism. And as a physician in later life, he would be the first to note the circulation of the blood, but—no surprise—biology was not to be his claim to infamy.

That claim began much earlier, when, as a lowly college student, he gained access to the Bible for the first time and actually read it for himself. What he found astounded him.

You see, he was not only smart, but he was also a man possessed of great compassion, and it pained him deeply to watch as the Spanish Inquisition bathed the streets in the blood of his Muslim and Jewish friends and neighbors. At sword-point they were ordered to confess faith in the Trinity or die. Devoutly religious people, most chose the sword. So imagine Servetus' amazement when he finally read the scriptures and found that it did not even mention the Trinity! In fact, there was nothing even remotely Trinitarian about it! This theological discovery, which had been kept from him his whole life, changed him forever.

"There is only one God," he exclaimed, that is all that the Bible teaches, and it is a belief shared by Jews and Muslims as well! "Hallelujah!," he thought. "Just wait until I tell the world! There is no need for bloodshed—the three religions can finally live together in peace, worshipping one God, the one of whom Moses, Jesus, and Mohammed all bore witness."

Servetus had rediscovered the ancient heresy of Arianism, all on his own, and became the father of a new religious community which endures to this day, and to which our beloved Robert and Elizabeth both belong: Unitarianism. Servetus wanted to share this discovery with everyone—there is only one God, not three. Jesus shows us God's face, but is just as human as we are! Servetus was sure that if he shared these discoveries with Calvin, Zwingli, and Luther, the Protestant churches would all embrace Unitarianism, and all faiths could live in peace and harmony.

But, oh, the idealism of youth! Of course, the Christian authorities did not take kindly to Servetus' discovery. The Protestant leaders likewise shunned him, and Servetus' life began to read like an espionage novel. He had to change his name, his profession, and move frequently to stay ahead of the Inquisition. He became a doctor at one point, a university professor at another, but all this time he continued to preach and write about his discoveries, and to critique the Catholic faith. He even sent a copy of Calvin's *Institutes* to Calvin himself with insulting comments in the margin. Remember, I said Servetus was academically brilliant, not that he had a half-thimble of horse-sense.

Finally, one jump ahead of the Inquisition, as usual, he fled to Geneva to take refuge with Calvin, who, he was sure, would forgive him for his insulting comments on the *Institutes*, and would surely embrace the Unitarian faith if Servetus could just talk to the man face to face.

Michael Servetus learned the hard way that old lesson, "Meet the new boss, same as the old boss." Calvin was no more tolerant of Servetus' teaching than the Catholics had been, and after a trial at a kangaroo court, Michael Servetus was sentenced to be burned at the stake. Not by the Inquisition, but by the Protestants, at the hands of the very man to whom he had come for help.

They tied Servetus to the stake and purposefully stacked very green wood around him. Green wood would burn hotter and slower, extending the heretic's agony and making plain to all God's just judgement on anyone who thinks for himself—except, of course, for Calvin! Before they lit the wood, they tied copies of Servetus' own books around his torso, so no one would miss the import of what was happening.

The bonfire was lit, and Servetus indeed died in great agony. He also died with the name of Jesus on his lips.

Not everyone in Geneva was keen to burn Servetus. One of Calvin's own lieutenants is known to have said of the event, "To burn a man is not to prove a doctrine; it is to burn a man!"

Calvin wanted to stamp out this heresy, but he did not, of course. Unitarianism thrived, especially in Transylvania, the most densely populated Unitarian area in the world, even today. But it was not just future Unitarians that would remember Michael Servetus. The good people of Geneva, although not sharing his faith, would honor his memory. For the Genevans later erected a statue in their town square, not to John Calvin, but ironically, to Michael Servetus.

His family back in Spain forced Michael's younger brother into the priesthood, and poured most of their money into the erection of a new church, hoping to redeem their name so besmirched by their heretical son. But today, we do not even know the name of the "good" son, it is the troublemaker we remember. It is Michael we honor today, and it is he to whom millions of Unitarians around the world look as the founder of their faith.

As Michael would be the first to tell us, rooting around in the church's history, or even reading scripture when you're not supposed to, can get you into a world of trouble. But his efforts set millions free to think for themselves, to worship a God their conscience can accept, to employ their labors for the betterment of society, and to alleviate the suffering of their fellow human beings. A little freedom, a little thought, a little rooting around in the basement can be a dangerous thing.

Fortunately for us, we live in a much more tolerant age. I am fortunate indeed that I can declare "I am a heretic" from this pulpit and still be warmly embraced at coffee hour. It speaks loudly of the freedom of thought and conscience we hold so precious in this parish.

As a preacher to this congregation, I feel it is my responsibility to think and speak freely. It is my responsibility not to give you the party line, but instead to spread out before you the rich feast of history, replete with tasty dishes no one has ever tasted before, not because I have any specific theological agenda to push, but because you are mostly adults, and even the children in our midst are encouraged to think for themselves. How can you choose what you will believe if you are not told of your options? In our church, no one is expected or required to espouse any specific doctrine: we ask only that you bring your whole selves to this table, your strengths, your doubts, your weaknesses, your heresies and your orthodoxies, all of them make us richer as a community. We are stronger because we differ, and we do well to encourage one another's diversities. In our community we are bound together not by what we believe, but by what we value: freedom, the sanctity of the individual conscience, and the bonds of holy friendship. Michael Servetus would have found a welcome place amongst us, and yet I fear he might have been even harder to preach for than Robert.

Spirit of the living God, the Maker of heaven and earth, in every age you send us prophets to call us into relationship with you. Help us to not be afraid to dig through the basement of our faith, and like your faithful servant, Michael Servetus, to speak the good news that we find there, even when such news is not popular. Give us a measure of his courage, as we strive, in every age, to be faithful to what you have made us to be. For we

*ask this in the name of everyone's favorite heretic, even Jesus Christ.
Amen.*

⊕ *Preached at Grace North Church July 22, 2001.*

18 | Paracelsus

A very good friend of mine, I'll call her Danielle, was a very successful businesswoman. She was a business coach, in fact, who made more money in one month than most of us see in a year. She worked hard for that money. Too hard, any reasonable person might say. Her over-commitment to her work resulted in a severe lack of attention to other areas of her life. Her relationships suffered. Her relationship to God suffered, and ultimately, her care of her own body, her needs for adequate rest and recreation, suffered. One day she fell so ill that she did not rise from her sickbed for six months.

For someone as driven as Danielle, this long period of inactivity was a living hell at first. Then, she began listening to the lessons her body had to teach her. She learned that the compulsive drive for "success" in the eyes of the business world was itself a sickness. The disregard with which our current business ethic holds the personal areas of our lives is itself a pandemic, and one which businesses and healthcare companies are only now starting to recognize.

As Danielle learned—and learned the hard way—a person needs to live a balanced life in order to be healthy. Time at work must be balanced with time for play, time for one's family and friends, time to rest, time to do art, and last but not least, time to meditate or pray.

Twenty years ago, such notions would have seemed laughable,

but more and more these days, health care organizations are turning their emphasis to prevention and holistic approaches to healthy living. There is even a wonderful magazine on the racks titled *Spirituality and Health* that takes as its founding premise that the two are inextricably linked.

Today's mystic, Paracelsus, was saying precisely the same thing 500 years ago, and if you thought these ideas were unpopular twenty years ago, you can just imagine the furor they raised during the Reformation.

Paracelsus was born Philippus Bombastus von Hehenheim in Einsiedeln, Switzerland, in 1493. He was the son of a physician, and surely the sight of his father giving medical aid to the pilgrims who flocked to the shrine in Einsiedeln made a deep and lasting impression on him.

As a young man, he studied medicine at the University of Vienna, with brief stints at various other universities, until he finally won his doctor's cap in 1515 at Ferrara. It was here that he adopted the name "Paracelsus" in the style of so many Renaissance gentlemen who styled themselves after the Greek and Roman men of letters they admired.

Paracelsus was a man possessed of an insatiable intellectual appetite. Having completed his formal studies in medicine, he went on to study metallurgy, chemistry, and alchemy, as well as traveling far and wide learning all he could about the healing arts. A fiercely peripatetic individual, he traveled to Spain, Portugal, France, England, across all of Germany, to Sweden and Moscow, and then through Poland, Austria, Hungary, Croatia, Italy, Crete, Constantinople, and finally Alexandria, Egypt. All this, believe it or not, in seven years.

What his travels instilled in him was a great disaffection with academia, and a much higher esteem for practical experience.

His practical experience served him well, as his reputation began to grow. In 1525 he was summoned to treat the famous Basel printer Johannes Froben, who had suffered a stroke. Under Paracelsus' care, the printer made a nearly miraculous recovery, and Paracelsus' fame grew even more. Leading intellectual lights began hanging out with him, and even Erasmus wrote him glowing letters lauding his medical prowess.

Thus it was that in 1526 the municipal council of Basel appointed Paracelsus the city *physicus*, which carried the added benefit of a chair at the local university, where Paracelsus shocked his students and the medical faculty by, of all things, lecturing in German. Academia recognized only Latin as the language of instruction, and although a mighty ruckus was raised, Paracelsus stuck to his guns and continued to teach in the vulgar tongue.

His undoing, however, was not far behind, as he had for some time been formulating his own theories about the cause and cure of diseases and had little patience with the ineffectual theories held in popular esteem in those days. He lashed out at the other professors and the ancient medical authors, calling them bunglers, fakers, liars, cheats, quacks, and even murderers and thieves! But the *pièce de résistance* was when he threw a revered classical textbook on medicine onto a bonfire in the public square. He was hauled into court, whereupon he turned his wrathful verbosity against the judge, the lawyers, the town council, and anyone else he could think of. His wrath is evident in his books as well, as one of them begins, "You authors of ancient texts, you will follow me, I will not follow you; you professors at the universities, you will follow me, not I you! Even in the remotest corner there will be none of you on whom the dogs will not piss. But I shall be monarch in my field, and mine will be the monarchy, and I shall lead the monarchy, so gird your loins!"

Conciliatory he was not. As a result of his public display of vitriol, the town ran him out, and a warrant was issued for his arrest.

Fortunately for our wily doctor, however, he escaped under cover of night, and his wanderings began anew. But this time, instead of simply recording his learnings, his writings as he traveled turned more and more to his own unique theories—theories which were more than 500 years ahead of his time.

Since we are all guilty of projecting our own ideas and our own inner realities onto the universe, and even onto God, perhaps Paracelsus can be forgiven for picturing God as the Great Physician, a kind of Paracelsus writ large. Like most Renaissance thinkers, Paracelsus was convinced of the interconnectivity of the microcosm and the macrocosm. This is the idea that the human body, the microcosm, is a perfect model of the universe itself, the macrocosm, and by paying attention to the body, we can learn all we need to know about the universe. Talk about projecting our own image onto the world!

As I said, this was a popular view in Paracelsus' day. His own innovation was seeing God as the macrocosmic physician, and human physicians as a kind of royal priesthood, whose holy duty it was to nurture and heal an imperfect and evolving creation.

And here is were Paracelsus' ideas are so profound: in a time when most people espoused the anti-cosmic sentiments of the church—the body is evil, the universe is corrupt, and so forth—Paracelsus countered that God intended humankind to collaborate with him. He intentionally made the world with the potential for perfection, but intentionally imperfect, for the very purpose of collaborating with humankind towards that great end. Thus the universe is not corrupt, human nature is not evil, and God is not a harsh taskmaster in Paracelsus' system. God is instead a friend and healer who longs for human companionship and requires human cooperation to complete his grand project.

But just how is this project to proceed? According to Paracelsus, God created the world in a state of imperfection, a mixture of divinity and dross. The work of humankind was identical to the work of the alchemists, only writ large, to separate the gold from the base materials through careful attention and scientific endeavor. Thus the *materia prima*, the unfinished, unpurified primal matter would someday be transformed into the *materia ultima*, perfected matter, where the soul and the body would be in perfect harmony; the microcosm and the spheres of the macrocosm would move in perfect synchronicity.

Since Paracelsus viewed humanity as being composed of three parts, physical, emotional, and spiritual, he believed that his system could lead to the eradication of all disease: physical, mental, and spiritual.

Disease, he felt, was caused by disharmonies in what he called the five *entia*, or entities. These *entia* are spheres of human endeavor that, until Paracelsus, were not thought of as being related. First there is the *ens astrorum*, or the historical field, containing the history and culture of a specific geographical place. Attention to place and to a people's culture is of utmost importance for one's health. The second *entium* is the *ens veneni*, the healthiness of one's food. Long before organic gardeners began warning us that toxic substances used in growing food could be dangerous to our health, Paracelsus was beating a similar drum. The third *entium* is the *ens naturale,* or the innate predisposition towards health or illness we are granted by our parents. In other words, Paracelsus took genetics into account in his schema. The fourth *entium* is the *ens spirituale,* or the field of social endeavor, as Paracelsus was convinced that the healthiness of our human interactions had a great effect on our health as well. Today, we might call this psychological health. The final *entium* is the *ens dei,* or that all-encompassing field that is God, for as Paracelsus tells us, our relationship to God is just as important to our well-being as any other aspect.

Loosely translated into modern terminology, then, Paracelsus believed that God and humankind were joined in a common goal, the perfection of the universe, which could only be brought about by attention to our healthy relationships with our past, the healthiness of the substances we put into our bodies, the genetic predisposition we have towards disease, our psychological well-being, and finally, a right relationship with God.

Unfortunately for our hero, the world was not ready to hear such a radical theory of health. They were, after all, still bleeding people and applying leeches. The idea that health is not about the treatment of disease, but instead is about healthy living in every area of our lives would take 500 years to filter into popular consciousness, and even now, poor Paracelsus is not given the credit he deserves as the great progenitor of this idea.

Unfortunately for Paracelsus, having to live his life on the road, literally fleeing for his life from place to place, he was not able to give proper attention to the *entia* he so powerfully extolled in his writings. And thus it was that in 1541 he suffered a fatal stroke, and amazingly, died in the good graces of the Catholic church. He was buried in the pauper's graveyard at the church of St. Sebastian in Salzburg, where his tombstone reads *"Vitam cum morte mutavit"* "He exchanged death for life."

Even though his main insights were to go ignored for half a millennium, his influence was vast. He deeply influenced generations of thinkers, including Jacob Bohme and Novalis. Soon, a cult of Paracelsus arose and numerous apocryphal books were written in his name, twisting his alchemical theories out of all recognition, and making him into a sort of pre-scientific messianic figure, one which Paracelsus himself surely would have despised.

Although as an academic Paracelsus was undoubtedly a failure, he was a great success as a philosopher, a physician, and a humanist, as, we are told, he never passed by a person in need without treating them, whether they could pay or not.

In one of his greatest works, he boldly asserted of his disparaging colleagues, "But I shall put forth leaves, while you will be dry fig trees." His prediction has come true. We no longer honor the theories of Galen or the other classical physicians, but we are just beginning to honor the holistic tradition so prophetically espoused by Paracelsus, the "Luther of Physicians."

Divine healer, when you walked among us you gave attention not only to those who were sick, but also those whom society oppressed, those who were infirm in mind, those whose relationships with family and fellow man were unhealthy, and especially those whose relationship with you was distorted; help us likewise to attend to all these needs. Minister to us, even as we minister to each other, that we may be whole in body and in soul. Amen.

⊕ *Preached at Grace North Church July 26, 2001.*

19 | Jacob Boehme

As has already been made painfully clear in this series, I spent my high school years as part of a fundamentalist church, an experience that wounded me significantly. No doubt I, in turn, wounded several others in service of this church and its monstrous god. I am not proud of that; I am only grateful that, fundamentalists though they are, my parents recognized that this church was so wacky it was unhealthy, and put in for a transfer to Benicia, California, to pry my sister and I from its clutches.

I was deeply wounded by this fundamentalist experience, as I said; so wounded, in fact, that not long after we moved I renounced my faith, my allegiance to the god of my parents, and everything to do with the church.

Of course, what this did was to leave me feeling even more acutely the spiritual vacuum in my life. Fundamentalism, I found out, could not quench my soul's thirst; and neither, as I quickly discovered, could sex, or drugs, or even rock-n-roll (although if anything came close, rock-n-roll did). And so it was that I found myself on my knees in my girlfriend's parking lot at four in the morning, blind stinking drunk, raging at the sky like King Lear in the storm. In the midst of my alcoholic, existential funk, I cursed the god of my parents, and pleaded with the universe, that if there were any *real* god, that he might be made known to me.

Well, be careful what you ask for. Twenty-four hours later I was speeding towards Disneyland with my girlfriend, Cherrisa, my best friend Bob, and his girlfriend, Sherry. Out of the blue, I asked, "Bob, what is God?" The answer I received was watershed.

While Bob was driving down Highway 5 he began casually describing the universe as a vast, seemingly chaotic, but infinitely intricate dance. All things in nature know their place in the dance; the angels, the demons, the planets, the stars, the rocks and trees, and animals. The only creatures who had forgotten how to dance were the humans. Our religious traditions, Bob said, were simply humankind's feeble attempts to get back in step with the dance.

The description hit me with the force of a vision; in fact my own memory of the event is positively psychedelic. While Bob described the dance, it unfolded before my eyes. Like the Buddha, I experienced a moment of *satori*, where for a fleeting flake of time I beheld the Great Truth of the universe, after which nothing would ever be the same. I cried for two days.

I went to Disneyland an atheist; I came back a universalist mystic. And how often do you hear that? I suppose I should keep quiet about it; it would give the Southern Baptist Convention just one more excuse to boycott Disney, I'm sure.

I have not had many visionary experiences. This one was my first, and certainly one of the most profound. I have no doubt that God orchestrated this little epiphany, using the hippie son of hippie parents with no theological pedigree to rock the world of this little ex-fundy, because God is a sneaky guy and has a great sense of humor.

Of course, people's lives are changed by visions and epiphanies all the time, even in times and places where having religious visions are not at all a popular thing to do.

One of these people who found their world turned upside down by a sudden encounter with divine truth was Jacob Boehme. Jacob was a shoemaker in Lutheran Germany, born in 1575. We know almost nothing of his early life, but we do know that when he was twenty-four, he caught the reflection of the sun in a polished pewter dish, and was instantly plunged into an ecstatic vision. Boehme later wrote, "…in one quarter of an hour I saw and knew more than if I had been many years together at a university." This unlearned man would spend the rest of his life attempting to describe, in feeble and limited human language, what he saw in that pewter dish.

Which, of course, makes it difficult for *me* to describe it to you. One reason for this is that Boehme was attempting to describe the ineffable, which always sets a mystical writer up for failure. But like most mystic writers, Boehme did not let the limitedness of his language deter him. He just tried, tried, and tried again. The thing is, every time he tried, he used different images, hoping that *this* time, he may get closer to actually being able to describe what he saw.

But the use of ever-different imagery makes it hard to tell you exactly what he *was* saying, since each interpretive lens took his metaphors in different directions. So to help me describe his system, I will borrow a set of images from a familiar source: C.S. Lewis' Chronicles of Narnia.

In the final Narnia book, *The Last Battle*, Aslan leads the Narnians through the door in the air to what he said was "the *real* Narnia," of which the Narnia they had for so long loved was but a pale reflection. The sage lion was right, the Narnians discovered: the light was brighter, the sun they knew could never have shone so brightly; the grass was of such a verdant hue that the grass they knew back in Narnia seemed dingy by comparison. And the waters that flowed in the streams made that mortal water they had always known seem like mere sludge. The Narnia they came from was almost exactly like the new Narnia, except that the old was now revealed to be only an inferior reflection of the *real* Narnia they were seeing now for the very first time.

Lewis did not get this part of his story from scripture, of course, but from Boehme, who, in that momentous vision caught in the pewter dish, saw that this world was not real as we imagine it to be, but only a real *reflection* of the divine reality.

He must have seen how the sun, reflected in the dish, appeared dimmer, distorted; the trees' colors washed together and lost their vibrancy. It is not hard to imagine the leaps his imagination took; for just as the sun in the dish was a dim reflection of the sun in the sky, so the sun in the sky was but a dim reflection of the sun as it shone in the divine reality.

Boehme asserted that although the reflection is not a perfect one, it is close enough for us to draw certain conclusions about the nature of the divine reality.

Boehme published his first book in 1612, titled *Aurora*, or *Day Dawning*, the first of his many attempts to describe his vision and its complex metaphysical implications.

All of this would have been fine had the pastor of Gorlitz, Martin Moller, not died about the same time as *Aurora* was published. For Moller was a mystic, and part of a movement away from strict Lutheran orthodoxy towards immediate mystical experience. Moller was a perfect mentor for Boehme. But Moller's successor, Gregory Richter, would prove to be his arch-nemesis.

Richter read Boehme's book, declared it heretical, had all copies confiscated, and banned Boehme from writing further.

Boehme obeyed, for a while. But soon the force of his unique vision compelled him to continue his attempts at description, and soon copies of new works from Boehme's pen began to circulate privately.

On New Year's Day 1624, Boehme's book of spiritual exercises, *The Way of Christ,* was published without his knowledge by a friend.

The publication of new heresies so enraged Pastor Richter that he attacked Boehme publicly from the pulpit, and the municipal council banished the mystical shoemaker from the city.

Richter died soon after, and Boehme, feeling his age and suffering from illness, returned to his beloved city.

The new pastor was much kinder to Jacob, and late in November 1624 he went to Boehme's home to hear his last confession and administer the Lord's Supper. On November 17th, Jacob Boehme breathed his last, and passed into the world of the Real with which he had been obsessed since catching his first glimpse of it so many years ago.

There are, as you might expect, many surprising elements to Boehme's teaching. One of the most astounding is his assertion that God can only be aware of himself when he manifests himself as an "other." In other words, God is incapable of self-reflection because there is nothing for God to reflect *upon.*

This pressure of desire, the desire to know and be known, became intolerable for God, and he became frustrated. This pressure resulted in movement, one could even say, an eruption of God. This motion outwards resulted an another mode of being for God, which could be beheld and interacted with. It was all still God, but it was not God in God's fullness, but an extension, a reflection of God.

The upshot of this is clear and is reminiscent of many mystical systems from Hinduism to Kabbala to Process Theology. God needs the material universe to achieve self-actualization just as much as the material universe needs God for its being and sustenance. God and creation are bound up in a waltz, a tango, an ecstatic dance in which all things in nature know their place except for us, much like Bob's revelation to John.

Another amazing implication of Boehme's system is that the process of creation is just that: a process. While people can be moral or immoral, processes are amoral. A process simply is; a gun, a newspaper, or an automobile are things, they are not moral or immoral in themselves. It is people who are moral or immoral in how they use these things. Just so, a process, like a piece of machinery, is amoral.

We see evidence of Boehme's process of creation everywhere we look. In the late fifties and early sixties, the Black community here in the United States longed to enjoy the rights and privileges promised them by the Constitution, but were frustrated from their desire by the enduring evil of racism. This frustration built up and built up until it erupted into movement: the civil rights movement. This movement resulted in the creation of a good thing, as America and the world woke up to the self-evident fact that had so eluded them: that all peoples are equal in the eyes of God.

The process was the same as Boehme's creation story: desire was frustrated, the resulting pressure erupted into movement, and this movement created something new.

As I said, this is an amoral process, but one that we can learn from. In the past few weeks we have seen this same process at work, with less happy results.

The Palestinians have been treated most unfairly by those in power in Israel. The Palestinian desire for a homeland, for the hope of living to their potential, for opportunities for their children, has been relentlessly frustrated. This frustration has reverberated throughout the Muslim world, added itself to other anti-American frustrations, and the collective pressure gained has erupted into our world with grave and malevolent force. I have no sympathy for the actions of the terrorists, but neither am I surprised by what has happened. Frustrated desire will always erupt, and a new thing will come into being.

We have yet to see what this new thing will be. Perhaps it will lead us into a horrific war; perhaps it is the bursting of a boil that brings our attention to the fact that the body of humanity is ill and needs healing. Perhaps Israel will repent of her sins against the Palestinians, perhaps this tragedy will result in a greater awareness of the humanity of our Muslim brothers and sisters and will facilitate greater dialogue and global healing. More likely a little of both will happen. But something will emerge, and I pray that after so much evil, something good may yet result.

Call me an optimist, if you must, but it is true that I have hope. I have hope that the religions of the world will realize their common attempts to get back in step with the divine dance of the universe; hope that nations will wake up to the violence they perpetrate against those living right next door to them; hope that in the end, the process of creation will always lead to beauty, truth, and goodness, in spite of the pain that birth always entails.

God of light, heat, and motion, instill in us a vision of Truth that will lead us to question the prevailing wisdom, courage to speak the Truths you reveal, and strength to endure those who assail us. For you "flame out, like shining from shook foil," or from a pewter dish, speaking to us in the sacredness of every present moment things which words are incapable of capturing. Help us, we pray you, to listen. Amen.

⊕ *Preached at Grace North Church September 30, 2001.*

20 | George Fox

How many of you have ever thought of yourself as a religious dissenter? A dangerous, unglamorous vocation; I'm not surprised there aren't many. The only time I could really claim such a mantle was when I was in college—and I thank God for college, because without it, I'd have precious few stories to tell from the pulpit!

In my second year at California Baptist College I had fallen in with a gaggle of freethinkers—or what passed for freethinkers at a fundamentalist school—known as the Socratic Club. We held socials, protests, art gatherings, and discussions, and not long after I joined we opened a coffeeshop on campus. We called it "The No Exit" after Satre's play, and as a bit of a warning to the preacher boys that they may be in danger of hellfire if they entered. The preacher boys—which was what we called the ministerial students—used to corner the incoming freshmen and warn them about the No Exit, and what would happen to their reputations if they went there.

But I do recall one time when I entered the No Exit and discovered four preacher boys in heated conversation with one of our Socratic members. They were arguing over the inerrancy of scripture. For a while I listened, and it occurred to me that arguing with such folk was futile; we were not going to convince them, they were not going to convince us. All our arguing generated, as the saying goes, more heat than light. At one point, however, I had a small revelation. Entering the fray, I opened my Greek New Testament to a random page and asked them to look at it. What they saw was approximately eight lines of text followed by the entire rest of the page which was nothing but footnotes; footnotes depicting variant readings in the most ancient manuscripts. "There are twenty variant readings for this verse alone," I pointed out to them. "Excuse me, but which one is the inerrant one?" Not another word was spoken. The preacher boys filed out, and I had won my first, and last, argument with a fundamentalist. I say it was the last because I swore that day I would never argue with another person over their religion again, and, as amazing as it might sound to you, I have kept that promise.

Much more enamoured of argument than I, however—and much more successful—was a young man named George Fox. Fox was born at a house named Fenny Drayton in Leicestershire in 1624, and lived his entire life in the shadow of the English Civil War. His father was a weaver, and like Jacob Boehme, Fox apprenticed as a shoemaker.

He never actually went to work as one, however. In 1643, at the age of nineteen, he found himself disillusioned with the Church of England, and he left his family behind, setting out on foot, like Siddhartha before him, to find the truth. After many hardships and much soul searching, he came to a mystical awareness of the Light within.

In 1647, he continued to roam the countryside, only this time he did so preaching, wherever he could find a crowd to hear him.

Unlike me, the young George Fox actually sought out arguments. He thought nothing of going into a church—for which he always used the pejorative term "steeple-house"—and interrupting the preacher in the middle of the sermon, contradicted him and challenged him to a debate. He was thrown out on his ear by more than one congregation, and eventually took to preaching an "alternative" sermon directly outside the steeple-house while the normal sermon was going on inside. For this and other disturbances he was thrown in prison, not once, but almost annually, certainly more times that we actually know about, where he invariably bore up with good humor and often converted—as he called it, "convinced"—his jailers to his way of thinking.

So just what were Fox's views that caused him so much trouble? First and foremost is the doctrine that the "Light of Christ" indwells every human being, and that this Light is the only reliable spiritual authority.

That doesn't sound too radical, you might be saying. In fact, it sounds rather common sense to us today, but in 17th-century England it was enough to put you away for treason! The implications of Fox's teachings rubbed almost everyone the wrong way.

For one thing, if the Light of Christ dwelt equally in all people, then all people were of equal value in the sight of God. This meant that in Quaker teachings, men and women were held in equal esteem and granted equal power and equal rights, right from the very beginning.

This doctrine also led Fox and his followers to reject the rigid classism of his day. Again like the Buddha before him, who insisted on the equality of all people and rejected the Indian caste system, Fox refused to acknowledge the various strata in society, and he did this chiefly by the use, or lack of use, of his hat. In the time and place where he lived, it was customary to take off your hat in the presence of someone of higher standing than you. If a merchant and a noble approached one another on the street, the merchant would remove his hat and show obeisance; women would do the same to men, and children to adults. But George Fox would have none of it and kept his hat firmly on his head even when enjoying his annual audience with the Lord Protector Oliver Cromwell. This insolence gained him a reputation as arrogant, but I think this was a perception of his enemies rather than a reality known by his friends.

Another implication of this doctrine of the Inner Light was that it alone was the sole spiritual authority. Not bishops, not priests, not ministers, not confessions, not creeds, not churches, not nations, and not even the Bible itself was considered an authority equal to the quiet whispering of the Light of Christ in the soul of every person.

Since the Church of England was a national church, and since one paid taxes to support it, Fox's denunciations of all churches, all ministers, and all bishops was nothing short of treason, let alone heresy.

Fortunately for Fox and his followers, it was a time of great religious upheaval. The last hundred years had seen England swing from Catholic to Anglican to Catholic again, back to Anglican, to

Puritan under Cromwell, and Anglican once again under the new King. Since lots of people had differing notions of just what kind of church should be the *one* church in England, people were more tolerant of dissenting voices. But then along comes George Fox, who says that *no* church is favored of God, and what are you going to do with that? People at that time were convinced that there should only be one state religion, and that society would fall apart if that were not upheld.

Quakers got no support from Puritans or other Protestants, either, for like us Baptist rebels in the No Exit, he rejected the inerrancy of scripture. While he found scripture helpful, and knew it better than most of his vocal sparring partners, he held a view— common in our day—that was almost unheard of in his own. The Bible, he taught, was the record of two peoples, the Israelites and the early Christians, and was their memory of their relationship with God. In other words, the Bible records what they remembered, not what actually happened, or even necessarily what God actually did or thought about the events. It was therefore a *human* document. We would say today that it *contains* the Word of God, but is not itself the Word of God. I like to think that Fox would have been proud of my one round of sparring with the preacher boys, but no doubt he would have found something to argue with me about as well; for instance, my conversion to Anglicanism, which I was going through at the time.

So not only did Quakers not support the state Church, not hold the Bible as a spiritual authority, and not recognize the obvious social strata so important to everyone around them, this doctrine of the Indwelling Light also moved them to become pacifists. For if God resides in everyone, how can we possibly kill one another? From the very beginning, then, Quakers were counter-cultural.

They were also, at least in the early days, exceedingly tolerant. If one lived one's life by the inner light, then truly one was free of all social constraints. The story is told of how, on one occasion, a man confronted George Fox in front of a crowd of people. He held his pipe out to Fox and bid him to smoke it, since he argued that those who follow the Light are free in all things. Now, you have to understand that tobacco had much of the same social stigma in Fox's day that marijuana has in our own, so everyone was watching closely to see what Fox would do. According to the account, Fox took the pipe from the man, held it to his lips for an instant, and then returned it to the man. Apparently George Fox, like Bill Clinton, did not inhale.

So if Quakers rejected steeple-houses, the authority of scripture, and the very idea of ministers, then what does religious life look like for a Quaker?

Quakers orient themselves, and everything in their lives, in honor of the Light within. Their worship services are called "meetings." In Fox's day, a meeting consisted of a bunch of Quakers sitting together in silence for an hour. If the inner light inspires someone to speak, they may speak. But speaking at length, and having more than three people speaking in any one service was frowned upon. Most Quaker worship consists of simply sitting in silence, listening for the gentle whisper of the Light within.

They did not call themselves Quakers, of course. Just as Christians were first given that name by their enemies, Quakers were called that for the first time by a judge, who meant it pejoratively, probably referring to the fact that some of Fox's followers actually shook in ecstasy when contemplating the Light within. Although Fox and his followers called themselves by a number of names during his preaching, such as "Friends of the Truth" or "Friends of the Light," Quakers eventually settled on The Society of Friends, possibly inspired by Jesus' assertion at the Last Supper that he called his followers not servants, but friends.

It was a name that fit them well, since Quakers have no hierarchy and are fiercely anti-authoritarian. They are all simply friends, with none greater than another.

This radical egalitarianism later brought Quakers to the forefront of the anti-slavery movement in the United States and has always moved Quakers to fight for peace, justice, and civil rights, often at the cost of their own lives.

Fox was truly an unstoppable man. Prison did not deter him, nor did inclement weather, nor his own health. Late in life he sailed to Barbados, and from there to New England, where he preached to record crowds. Finally, in 1691, at the age of 66, he succumbed to poor health and what was at the time a ripe old age, dying peacefully at home, surrounded by his Friends.

Those who came after him definitely inherited his mantle, traveling far and wide and preaching the Light of Christ in the face of deadliest peril.

Even during Fox's own lifetime, one woman named Mary Fisher traveled to the Mediterranean, escaped the clutches of the Inquisition, gained entry into Turkey, and managed to set up an interview with the Sultan of Turkey in his own army headquarters. She preached to him about how the Light was common to all peoples and how Islam and Quaker Christianity had much in common. Her message was well received, and she returned to England in safety. Others were not so fortunate. One Quaker set out to convert the Pope and died at the hands of the Inquisition.

The early Quakers kept voluminous journals, and so their beginnings are better documented than most religious movements. One amazing story tells how a ship full of Quakers set sail from Europe to America without a navigator! They were certain that the Light within would not steer them wrong, and even many of their own number in the colonies were amazed when their ship sailed into Boston Harbor in record time.

Today, there are approximately 240,000 Quakers in the world; about 120,000 of these are Americans. When you remember that there are approximately 6 million Lutherans in the US alone, this is a very small number, and their influence has far exceeded their size. Quakers were instrumental in ending slavery in the US and England, and though they refuse to fight in wars, the Quaker Ambulance Service has been in the thick of many of them, providing first aid and taking the wounded of either side to safety.

In the US, Quakers differ greatly. Some of them keep to the old traditions of worshiping in silence, while others have adopted many of the practices of their Protestant neighbors, hiring pastors and using hymns in their worship. But any Quaker meeting will include some time for silence, for introspection, and for listening to the Inner Light.

I would like to invite you to join me in a bit of Quaker practice. In lieu of a meditational prayer, I invite us all to sit in silence for only five minutes. During this time, let us contemplate the Light of God that lives within each one of us. And if we can still our own thoughts, quiet our own hearts, and listen carefully, perhaps we will hear a word from God, too.

⊕ *Preached at Grace North Church October 21, 2001.*

21 | Emmanuel Swedenborg

In the mid 1940s, my grandmother died. Briefly. She was giving birth to my aunt Reta, and due to complications during the pregnancy, her heart stopped, and they thought they had lost her. While the doctors were frantically trying to revive her, my grandmother was having an adventure completely unseen to those standing over her body in the delivery room.

According to her, she was transported to a lush green pasture, through which a swift stream wound its way. There was a white bridge spanning the stream, and standing on the bridge were many people my grandmother knew and loved. Her own grandmother was there, and many others whom she recognized that had passed on.

But the most wonderful part of the experience was that she was met on this side of the river by Jesus himself. He told her not to be afraid, that everything was going to be all right. He also told her that it was not yet her time, and that she must return and raise her children.

My grandmother did not want to leave Jesus' side, she longed to cross the bridge and enter into her heavenly reward, but she also knew that it would not be permitted, and resigned to returning to earth, she agreed and came back.

Ever since this experience, my grandmother has been absolutely certain of her eternal reward, talks about Jesus and heaven incessantly, and sings hymns night and day. She is most insufferable.

But her certain hope in her Lord is also as enviable to me as it is strong. I wish I had half the faith she does. Perhaps if I had died, met God, and returned, I would not be such an agnostic. Perhaps the same is true of you.

Her experience is not unusual, of course. Thousands of people have had what we now call "near death experiences," and amazingly, they are startlingly similar in detail. The problem is that people do not get very far in their journeys to the other side before being told to return. I know of only one person who has explored the worlds beyond in much greater detail—Emanuel Swedenborg.

Born on January 29th, 1688, in Stockholm, Sweden, the young Swedenborg was raised in a loving and pious home. His father was a seminary professor who entreated young Emanuel constantly to love and serve God. His mother, unfortunately, died when he was only eight years old, but not before she had given birth to six young siblings.

His father was later consecrated a Lutheran bishop who served as private chaplain to the Swedish royal family. He was then granted nobility, and so their name was changed from Swedberg to Swedenborg. I would be grateful if anyone here could explain to me the distinction at coffee hour. In any case, it seemed important to them, and for the rest of his life, young Swedenborg would move in the highest social circles in the land.

A voracious student, Swedenborg studied philosophy and mastered English, Dutch, French, and Italian, as well as Greek, Hebrew, and Latin, all before he was twenty years old. To relax, he wrote poetry in Latin, and learned the organ well enough to substitute at church when the regular organist was away.

At twenty-two years of age, he travelled to England, where he studied physics, astronomy, and the other natural sciences. He also mastered several practical crafts, including watchmaking, bookbinding, cabinet work, engraving, and brass musical instrument construction. From there he went to Holland, where he added lens grinding to his resume.

His later academic studies included cosmology, mathematics, anatomy, physiology, politics, economics, metallurgy, mineralogy, geology, mining engineering, and chemistry. By the time he was thirty-five, Swedenborg had learned most of what the academic world had to offer and can be safely said to be one of the most highly educated men in the world in his time.

Even before his travels ended, at the age of twenty-eight, the King of Sweden appointed him to be extraordinary assessor of the Royal College of Mines, a position he took seriously, riding far and wide, inspecting safe and unsafe mines, handling administration, hiring, firing, and arbitrating disputes. Not long after, he took his father's seat in the House of Nobles where he helped to govern the country for over fifty years.

None of this would be terribly remarkable if all of this learning and influence had born no fruit, but Swedenborg was indefatigably creative. In the royal service, Swedenborg designed dry docks, machinery for working salt springs, an airplane, a submarine, a steam engine, and a slow-combustion stove.

His acumen in anatomy far exceeded the accepted dogma of the day, and his writings include the first accurate understanding of the cerebral cortex and the respiratory movement of the brain tissues.

In 1713, King Charles II asked him to solve a very difficult problem. The King needed to transport five warships over fifteen miles of dry land, as he was at war with the Danes. Swedenborg instantly came up with a design and completed the project in under seven weeks.

According to Colin Wilson, "All of this practical work starved the religious side of his nature, and in 1744 this burst out like a torrent." It all started with a dream, which featured a roaring wind that picked him up and flung him on his face. In his dream, he started to pray, and then suddenly Jesus was standing in front of him. They had a conversation, which ended with Jesus saying, cryptically, "Well, then, so..." and then he woke up.

Thereafter, he would lapse frequently into ecstatic trances, during which he said he left his body and travelled to other worlds. He claims to have explored Heaven and Hell extensively, and wrote volume after volume documenting his conversations with angels.

Which, of course, is why we are speaking about him today. Swedenborg's revelations about the next world represent the most comprehensive literature on the next life we possess. It is certainly the most detailed, and is definitely the most voluminous.

According to Swedenborg, all beings are useful, and this doctrine of "usefulness" is an important one in his system. Beings are useful not simply on earth, but after their death as well. Those who have died and passed over live much as we do. They dwell in houses, live in familial units, have jobs, go on vacations, and continue to better themselves through education and experience.

Furthermore, there is no great judgement. God does not send a soul to Heaven or Hell. Souls seek their own levels, and a soul will naturally gravitate towards the place he or she feels most comfortable. Those of you who have seen the Robin Williams movie, *What Dreams May Come,* have seen a near-perfect description of the Swedenborgian afterlife.

Swedenborg's revelations were not well received by his contemporaries, which probably does not surprise you. For one thing, he rejects the doctrine of Jesus' vicarious atonement on the cross, saying that God does not need atonement since God is neither vindictive nor petty. God, in Swedenborg's system, is Divine Goodness, and Jesus is Divine Wisdom, and since Goodness must be approached through Wisdom, so do Christians approach God through Jesus.

He also propounded a system of correspondences. Like many others of his time, Swedenborg believed the occult doctrine, "As above, so below," and taught that everything on earth corresponds to a spiritual reality. Not only that, but that the human is a map of the universe, and that everything in nature has a correspondence to something pertaining to the human being.

This is very Platonic and Hermetic, of course, but Swedenborg's genius was in applying this principle to his reading of scripture. The Bible should be read on two levels, Swedenborg taught; the surface, literal meaning, and a symbolic, spiritual meaning.

If you are thinking, "Wow, that sounds remarkably like Origen's system of biblical interpretation," you are quite correct—it is frighteningly similar.

Take for example the puzzling verses in the book of Revelation describing the four horsemen of the Apocalypse. The section is difficult to understand, and most people read the horsemen to be symbols of various times of trial to be visited upon humankind at the end of the world. But not so with Swedenborg. In his system, the horse corresponds to the human intellect. The four horsemen represent the declining influence of human intellect on spiritual matters in the four ages of the church's history. The white horse represents the undiluted truth expounded by the apostles at the beginning of the church's history. The red horse who wielded a sword and took peace from the earth represents the church's will corrupted by passion and hatred, perhaps during the Constantinian era. The black horse represents the complete perversion of the Christian intellect, and the pale horse represents his current culture's complete lack of spiritual understanding.

Though many of Swedenborg's correspondences seem arbitrary, a close reading will reveal a remarkably clever and predictable pattern which can be mastered by anyone willing to put the time and effort into pouring through his almost endless stream of writings.

For most of this time, Swedenborg published his spiritual writings anonymously. But word got out one night when his mystical visions showed him something so frightening he could not master himself. On July 19, 1759 a great fire broke out in Stockholm. Swedenborg was a guest at a dinner party three hundred miles away at the time, where he announced with great dismay that a fire had just broken out. Two hours later, he announced with great relief that it had been extinguished just three houses before his own. Two days later a messenger arrived from Stockholm with news which confirmed every detail of Swedenborg's vision.

The cat was out of the bag, and people far and wide soon began to appeal to him for his clairvoyant services. Even the Queen summoned him and asked if he had seen or talked with her brother, the Prince Royal of Prussia, who had passed on not long before. He told her he had not, but would say hi for her if he did. The next time Swedenborg appeared at the royal court, he strode boldly forward and approached her majesty. Swedenborg gave her greetings from her brother, and also passed along her brother's apologies for not answering her last letter before he died. He then relayed the contents of a posthumous letter, which he was under orders from the departed Prince to do. The Queen was overwhelmed, and wondered aloud, "Nobody could possibly have known these things."

Amazing as Swedenborg's powers as a medium were, and as insightful a theologian as he was, we cannot accept any of his writings uncritically. Like any sacred text, his writings are a product of his time and couch eternal truths in ephemeral forms. Plus, there were the things Swedenborg said which were simply dead wrong, such as his assertion that most of the planets in the solar system are inhabited, that the citizens of the moon speak from their stomachs instead of from their lungs (and therefore their speech sounds like belching), or that Martians have faces which are half black and half tawny, live on fruit and dress themselves with tree bark.

Nonetheless, he had a remarkable influence on many important people. Johnny Appleseed not only spread appleseeds far and wide, but the reason for his travels was that he was a Swedenborgian evangelist, and planted more Swedenborgian tracts than he did apple seeds. William Blake was among those followers who first helped to organize a Swedenborgian church—something Swedenborg himself never recommended. Perhaps his most famous disciple was Helen Keller, who was a devout Swedenborgian until her death. Her book *My Religion* is still widely read, and contains a detailed, if highly hagiographic, account of his life.

Of course, there were those who hotly opposed the doctrines he taught. He was formally charged with heresy, and the Royal Court condemned his heresy and banned his books. Swedenborg appealed to the King, and the issue went to the Court of Appeals, where it ended in a hung jury due to a legal stalemate. Swedenborg was left alone to continue his writing and publishing until his death.

Not long before he died, Swedenborg invited John Wesley, the founder of Methodism, to visit him, as he knew Wesley was interested in his writings, and he hoped they could have a fruitful discussion of theology. Wesley was surprised as he had told no one of his fascination with Swedenborg. He told Swedenborg he would be passing through and would drop in on him in six months. Swedenborg wrote back saying that would be too late, as he would be passing into the world of the spirits on March 29, 1772.

Which is exactly what he did. At five o'clock in the afternoon on March 29th, at the ripe old age of 84, he asked his maid what time it was. He was told, and replied, "It is good. God bless you." And then made his final journey to the spirit world, this time to stay. Swedenborg now rests in public view in the Cathedral of Uppsala in Sweden, an honor reserved for kings, bishops, and generals.

What he left behind is an amazing kaleidoscope of biblical exegesis and spiritual exploration. Many of his original manuscripts still survive because the snuff he was addicted to and used constantly acted as a preservative. Two churches bear his name; the more fundamentalist of the two is episcopal in polity, and the more liberal is congregational. If you have not visited the Swedenborgian Church building in San Francisco, I recommend making a point of it, as it is a very beautiful building indeed.

What are we to make of his sometimes bizarre visions? Most liberal Swedenborgians view them in a more or less Jungian fashion, as articulations of timeless archetypes to be interpreted, not taken literally. This is a sensible way to proceed with Swedenborg, and I heartily recommend exploring him further. The Swedenborgian Society is still very active and keeps all of his works in print, in some very nice editions indeed. Swedenborgian study groups meet in every major city, even where there are not Swedenborgian churches, and his ideas continue to influence the intellectual and spiritual life of humankind.

But perhaps his greatest gift is that of comfort. For aside from Jesus, he is the only person who has explored the worlds beyond and returned to tell about it. Perhaps much of his information is the product of his own very active imagination, but then again, he has a very good track record, and his descriptions match in almost every detail the witness of those who, like my grandmother, have had near-death experiences.

This week saw the passing of one of our most beloved parishioners, Col. Harvey Short. As I was preparing this sermon this week, I felt Harvey's presence profoundly and found Swedenborg's descriptions of the next world to be very comforting indeed. If Swedenborg is correct, then Harvey is settling into his new place, and fixing it up for the time when his beloved bride will once again sleep beside him. I would like to think that Harvey is once again gainfully employed teaching students from his great store of knowledge. I won't know for sure until I cross that white bridge myself. But until then, I will be content to take Swedenborg's word for it. After all, who else has been there? Who else can say but him?

Supreme teacher, you are indeed our path to God. For it is through knowledge of the Divine that the Divine is known, and we never stop learning, in this life or the next. Teach us in this present classroom, and lead us to the next, where our learning may be increased, our insatiable appetite for knowledge fed, and our hearts find rest. For we ask this in the name of the one Swedenborg called Holy Wisdom, even Jesus Christ. Amen.

⊕ *Preached at Grace North Church June 2, 2002.*

22 | Georg Friedrich Hegel

Brahman, the one God, had just seen to it that Indra and the other gods won their latest battle. Indra and the others were taking credit, bragging about their bravery and ferocity when Brahman appeared to them. They were a bit taken aback and said to each other, "Who is this being that fills us with such awe?" They pushed Agni out in front and told him to find out (he was, after all, supposed to know everything).

"Who are you?" asked the One God. "I am the god of fire," Agni answered. "What power do you possess?" Agni replied proudly, "I can burn all things on the earth." Brahman placed a piece of straw before him and said, "Burn this." Agni tried and tried, but couldn't even raise a decent smolder. Agni returned to the other gods shaken and bewildered.

Next the gods sent Vayu, the god of the air. "I am Vayu, god of air and space," he announced when he stood in front of the mysterious being. "What are your powers?" Brahman asked. "I can carry off all the earth in a whirlwind." Brahman held forth the same piece of straw and said, "Blow this away." Vayu too, returned unsuccessful.

Finally Indra, chief of the gods, squared his jaw and ran toward the being, but Brahman disappeared. All the gods were speechless with wonder, for they knew they had seen the Supreme Spirit, the source of their being.

This myth from the Hindu tradition was herald to a paradigm shift in Indian culture. On one level, it is the story of how a strict polytheism gave way to an all-inclusive monotheism; it is the story of how humans began to think of God differently. On another level, however, we see in this story God's self-revelation, not just to humans, but to himself; it is therefore the unfolding of God's self-knowledge, albeit in human terms, and utilizing human mythology.

When you think about it, though, how could it be otherwise? All revelations of God are voiced by humans, and couched in human cultural terminology. There has never been a divine revelation that has been completely new, utterly divorced from the human culture that gave it expression. But why should this be so if the divine is a separate being that lives outside the cultural sphere of humans? Why could God not simply tell us the unmitigated truth, unobscured by myth or culture?

I'm not sure that this is a question that Georg Friedrich Hegel actually set out to answer, but it is a question that his philosophy helps to answer, nonetheless. And of course you may be asking, "Wait a minute, I thought this series was about heretics and mystics, not philosophers," but I beg your indulgence, for as we shall see, philosophy and theology are two sides of the same coin, one side approaching the divine via the book of scripture, and the other side approaching the absolute via the book of nature. And in Hegel's case, it is even more obscure, for he began his studies as a theologian, and according to many of his critics, never really left that study.

Hegel was born in 1770, in Stuttgart. The eldest of three children, his father was a minor financial official in the court of the Duchy of Württemberg. His childhood was, by all accounts, unremarkable, except when he lost his mother at the age of eleven. At eighteen he began attending the theological seminary, since his professors said he had no facility in philosophy. After he graduated he supported himself as a private tutor. These were some pretty rough times for the young Hegel, and led him to write to a friend, "I have made my guiding star the Biblical saying, 'Seek ye first food and clothing, and the kingdom of heaven shall be added unto you.'"

Soon after his father died, leaving him enough money to stop tutoring and spend his time lecturing. After three years of freelance lecturing, he was finally granted a teaching post—in philosophy, naturally.

For many years he taught at the university in Jena, where he began working on his first important book, *The Phenomenology of Spirit*. This was a time of great personal turmoil for Hegel, as news of Napoleon's approaching armies filled the air with dread, and he had just discovered that his secret lover, Christina Burkhard, was pregnant with his child. The very day he finished his book, October 13, 1806, Napoleon's army overran the little university town. Just as the French soldiers were beating down his front door, Hegel fled out the back, clutching to his breast the only copy of his just-completed manuscript.

In fleeing Jena, Hegel escaped both harm and palimony and went on to write a good many other books, which, according to Will Durant, "captivated Germany by [their] unintelligibility." Indeed, this is one of the chief complaints about his writing; his staggering verbosity served only to obfuscate rather than illuminate what he was trying to say. Once someone asked him to summarize his philosophy in one sentence, and he replied with ten volumes.

I, however, have only about ten minutes remaining before your patience runs out, and so I shall attempt to do what Hegel would—or could—not. I'm still not going to get it down to a sentence, but nor, I hope, will it tax your patience.

Hegel's philosophy has its origins not in logic, but in a flash of mystical insight. It occurred to him very early on that the universe was just one thing. Now this is indeed a perspective common to all the great mystics, but not necessarily a popular starting point for philosophers. Hegel would spend the rest of his career trying to reconcile his mystical vision with the demands of logic.

In doing so, he did us a great favor, though the fruits of his labor took some time to be appreciated. His philosphy was, in a way, the first critique of the "parts" mentality so universally espoused by the modern project. While all around him burgeoning scientists were breaking reality down into its constitutive elements to see what makes them tick, Hegel warned us to take a step back and see the whole picture. "Only the whole is real," he tells us. Everything we are looking at must be seen in terms of its relationship with everything else, otherwise our view is distorted. This is a remarkably postmodern perspective, and resonates with many contemporary philosophies such as chaos theory and the Gaia hypothesis.

Hegel even provides us with a creation myth of sorts that further illuminates his system. According to Hegel, in the beginning God was pure mind, pure being. Since God was alone, God attempted to think about Godself; after all it was dreadfully dull, and as God was the only subject *and* the only object in existence, what else would God have to do? Unfortunately, the thought of pure being is impossible, apparently even for God, so when God tried to think about Godself, God thought about nothing instead. Actually God thought about no-thing, the very opposite of being.

But since God *is* God's thought, God's failure to comprehend Godself resulted in an internal distance being created. Hegel calls this God's self-alienation. This appears in our mythology as the figure of Satan, God's self-alienated essence and the opposite of God's pure being. This alienation proved to be quite catastrophic for God, who has spent most of the life of the universe trying to reconcile God to Godself. Are you still with me?

So what we have here is a God of two minds who can't seem to get it together. God can neither recapture the womb-like coziness of pure being, nor can God be content with annihilation. All of history then falls somewhere in between, a vast space Hegel terms "becoming." All the universe participates in this "becoming." In fact, the project of the universe, according to Hegel, is to re-acquaint God with God's self. Apparently, in trying to think about Godself, God lost Godself, and the whole vast drama of history is God's attempt to remember who God was. So let that be a lesson to you not to be too self-absorbed.

Those of you with an interest in world religions will recognize this as a kind of Western Hinduism. The universe exists only as a way for God to rediscover God's self. In Hinduism, however, this self-revelation is intentional and playful; the universe is God's playground. But in Hegel's system, there is an element of desperation involved. God's self-alienation is an extremely uncomfortable state for the almighty, and God is not only not playful, but is not at all happy about the situation. Not only that, but it is taking way too long to sort this little mess out. But according to Hegel, that is God's problem; for us, it's just the neighborhood we have to live in.

Hidden in this creation myth is Hegel's great gift to human thought, what we now call the "Hegelian dialectic." God's pure "being" was the thesis, God's subsequent thought of "no-thing" was the antithesis, and the resultant, ongoing process of "becoming" is the synthesis. This process, "thesis, antithesis, synthesis," Hegel subsequently applied to everything, from politics to history to religion, and in doing so he revealed history not as a static list of events but as a dynamic process in which every action is connected to the movement of the whole, every element is affected by every other element, and each event is formed and informed by those that have gone before it.

It is easy to see how helpful this insight was. Suddenly history made a whole lot more sense. Even biology finds this expression useful. On this Father's Day we might do well to recall that if Daddy is thesis and Mommy is antithesis, baby is the synthesis born of their interplay. Even when applied to our own smaller stories, the dialectic yields results. For instance, my own spiritual journey makes more sense and hangs together as a whole when thought about in terms of Hegel's theory. I began my religious journey as a Southern Baptist, a denomination which stresses individualism and congregational polity. In college I was converted to Catholicism, the very antithesis of my childhood faith in that it stresses communal life and is hierarchical in polity. After many years, God led me to this parish, where thesis and antithesis have formed a synthesis we here call "congregational catholicism" which preserves the best of both worlds, being both communal and self-governing. Thesis, antithesis, synthesis.

It is not hard to see this simple, trifold pattern, and I invite you to explore your own history with this dialectic in mind. It may yield some surprising insights, or as I prefer to call it, "great stuff to work on in therapy."

Now, Hegel may have thought that he had described the very pinnacle of human thought, but unfortunately, he was a stone's-throw too clever for his own good. For his system contains a built-in mechanism for its own obsolescence: if Kant is the thesis, and Hegel is the antithesis, well, even Hegel should have seen it coming; soon the very philosophers he was teaching would provide the synthesis that would render Hegel more of a footnote than king-of-the-hill, as we shall see in our next sermon on Kierkegaard.

But Hegel's groundbreaking work certainly won him fame in his own day. In 1818 he accepted a prestigious post in Berlin, and even had a national holiday declared in his honor. His dialectic was all the rage, and even while his fellows were still shaking their heads over the gawd-awful mess he called a systematic philosophy, the world had decided he was a genius. While he was a left-wing revolutionary as a young man, the end of his life saw him turning his energies to political philosophy in service of the Prussian government, and his final book *The Philosophy of Right* was both right-wing and very conservative indeed. He died in 1831, and many of his lectures were later compiled and published posthumously.

Now you may be thinking that this is all very interesting—or not—but what does all of this mean for us as modern-day people of faith? Hegel's philosophy has been extremely important in the development of various theological and philosophical movements, some of which you will hear about as this sermon series progresses. But more importantly, Hegel's system reveals to us that we, we small beings, are the organs of God's self-revelation. According to Hegel, God can conceive neither of pure being nor pure non-being. Which not only put all of us here in the middle, but set us up with a daunting task: to reconcile God to himself through the unfolding of history. In other words, you are an essential element in forming the being that God is in the process of becoming. To put this another way, it is not God who is our savior, it is we who are God's.

Now you can participate in this becoming willingly; otherwise you will most assuredly participate in it unwillingly, for it is not something you can really escape. After all, where would you go? But the best option is to participate in it consciously, to see yourself as related to the Whole, to see that the life of the universe, the life of God, is affected by the decisions *you* make and the degree of consciousness you bring to your own process of becoming.

You can, of course, elect to reject God, or ignore God, but that will not stop The Being Who Fills Us with Wonder from coming. You can pontificate and bluster like Agni and Vayu, but that will not threaten the Being Who Fills us with Wonder. On the other hand, you can be like Indra, who charges full speed towards the Being, and discover that it is only yourself, or more accurately, that its life is your life, and that the two are inseparably bound together; they are, in fact, one and the same thing.

Hegel thus calls us to participate consciously in the evolution of God. For God's story is not done; indeed, one could say it has barely begun. Nor is God's end assured. Whether or not God ever achieves his goal of complete self-knowledge or re-integration depends largely on our cooperation. For it is only in the minds of self-reflexive beings that God becomes self-aware, it is only in your imagination that God is aware of his own existence, his purpose and goal, and it is only through your efforts that that goal may be realized. Or you can blow it all off and go get a burger. But remember that for every grand thesis and mundane antithesis there is a profound synthesis. We can both chow down *and* discuss philosophy, which, personally, is my favorite way to spend a lunch.

You, O God, are the being that fills us with wonder. Help us to grasp the great truth that your servant, Hegel calls us to: that your life and our life are one and the same epic story; that how we view ourselves and our role profoundly affects you, and that nothing in the universe is an island. Move through us with thy holy wisdom, help us to be conscious of the Whole so that as we evolve and grow into increasing health and complexity we may be aware that it is not only ourselves that benefit and suffer. All beings are connected, and all are in the service of your unfolding Self. Help us to help you, even as we strive to survive and love each other. For we ask this in the name of the one who first loved us, even Jesus Christ. Amen.

⊕ *Preached at Grace North Church June 2, 2002.*

23 | Søren Kierkegaard

Our opening reading from Genesis (chapter 22) is a famous and deeply troubling myth: Abram hears God's call and decides to follow. Because of his faith he is granted a new identity—Abraham—and finds a deeper, more coherent and meaningful life with a moral center. Abraham and his wife Sarah are childless until their old age, when Sarah, miraculously, gives birth to their son Isaac. "Isaac" means laughter, because Sarah thought it was so funny that someone as old as she could be pregnant. But pregnant she was, and Isaac was born, a healthy and thriving baby.

But then, God does something inexplicable. He demands that Abraham take his only son—the miracle child of his old age—up to the top of the mountain, and sacrifice him to God. Against all reason, Abraham agrees, and leads his unsuspecting child up the mountain. When they arrive, he ties up his son, and raises the knife for the kill. Just then, an angel stays his hand, and Isaac is saved. God didn't *really* want Isaac to die, the story says, he only wanted to see if Abraham would go through with it.

In the eyes of the writer of Genesis, this makes Abraham a giant of faith; to the rest of us, well, he should probably be locked up for attempted murder. Most of us, especially those who are parents, can muster some outrage at this story, and insist that Abraham *should* have declined and therefore rendered himself God's moral superior. After all, what kind of monster would insist on the murder of a child? Even when it is revealed to be a "test," God is at the same time revealed to be a cruel and capricious trickster.

That is how we see things in the early 21st century, but previous generations have not seen this story in such black and white terms. To us, Abraham seems a criminal; but for multitudes of generations, he is held up as a great hero.

Our current mystic, Søren Kierkegaard, certainly saw him as such. He sees within the story of Abraham a paradigm for psychological, spiritual, and moral development that all thinking people should emulate. This does not mean we should construct stone altars and start sharpening our knives. Instead, Kierkegaard has something much more abstract, and at the same time, more concrete, in mind.

Søren Kierkegaard was born in Copenhagen, Denmark, on May 5, 1813. He was the youngest son of seven children, and was, like Isaac, born in his parents' old age. His father was 56 when he was born, not exactly old, but pretty far along for a new baby. His mother died when he was a teenager, and though he seemed to be very fond of her, it was his father who was to profoundly shape his inner life.

His father was a hard, pious man, often extremely depressed, and espousing a severe version of Christianity. Søren himself says, "As a child I was strictly and earnestly brought up to Christianity, humanly speaking, insanely brought up: even in my earliest childhood I had been overstrained by impressions which were laid upon me by the melancholy old man who was himself oppressed by them—a child, insanely travestied as a melancholy old man."

Søren recognized that his father's severity in religion made him, Søren, old before his time, and at the same time he rebelled against this form of religion, and was subsumed by it. He studied theology in college and always considered himself a theologian more than a philosopher. He is, perhaps, wrongly identified as a philosopher, since all of his wrestlings are religious ones, and he professed his commitment to Christ to his death.

Even though he revered the patriarch Abraham, and perhaps saw a little of his own father in him, his own dilemma was not nearly so dramatic. Kierkegaard's own drama begins—as it so often does—with a girl.

In 1840, Søren asked Regine Olsen to marry him. He had had a crush on her for about a year, and to his great surprise, she accepted. This was the beginning of a roller coaster ride that would last the rest of his life. For no sooner had she accepted than Søren was afflicted with a near-terminal case of cold feet. He blamed it on his melancholy. It was burden enough for one person, how could he ever subject another person to it? Hadn't he suffered enough under his father's depression? How could he turn around and do the same to another?

So he decided he must break off the engagement, but in his day, to do so would bring shame upon his beloved. So he thought it would be best if she broke up with him. But instead of coming to her like a normal, decent person, and telling her what was troubling him, Søren goes the TV sitcom route and decides to act like a total buffoon in public until she gives up on him and gives him back his ring. What follows is likewise sitcom fodder. She sees right through his ruse, and loves him anyway.

Disgusted with himself—and rightfully so—Søren finally breaks up with her, and in the fashion of romantic young men everywhere, decides that from here on out he could either be only a wild libertine or an ascetic. He chooses the latter, and spends the rest of his life writing about his broken heart and self-imposed exile. But just when you think, "Good God, Søren, get over yourself," he takes this petulant acting out and uses it as fodder for deep reflection and changes the trajectory of Western thought. "For the want of a nail" as they say, or in his case, a girlfriend.

Kierkegaard was an enthusiastic Hegelian in college, but became a fierce critic of Hegel after his experience with Regine. For him, Hegel's positing of some grand all-encompassing system was sheer fantasy. How does Hegel know that "only the whole is real" or that "the real is the rational"? These were not provable assertions. "The real" in Kierkegaard's own experience was absurd, not rational. And besides, there is no way we can know the "whole"; we can only theorize, which makes Hegel's theory about as firm a foundation to build on as Rapunzel or Hansel and Gretel.

Besides, in Hegel's system, all decisions and directions are subsumed into a dialectic. It doesn't matter what one does because an antithesis will follow, and a synthesis will mitigate the effects of both. In Hegel's system, not only is the individual denied sovereignty over his own life, but the very notion of oneself as an "individual" is illusory, since each person is only a cell in the great body of the whole.

Kierkegaard denied the whole kit and caboodle. Instead, he said that philosophy stops and starts with the individual and each individual's personal experience. He defined two types of knowledge which impact us. First is objective knowledge, which everyone knows and is more or less provable, like mathematics, or the changes of the seasons. Objective knowledge is important, but it does not define me. The second type of knowledge, however, does. This is subjective knowledge, the type of knowledge that a person can only know for him or herself.

Kierkegaard titled his first book as a slap in Hegel's face. It was called *Either/Or*, and you'll notice there is no synthesis emerging from these two choices. Kierkegaard insisted that we are free to make our own decisions, and that these decisions have profound consequences. We cannot allow ourselves to get lost in some theory, we must instead attend to the very real hard knocks that life throws at us, and tend to how these shape us as personalities, as individuals. Hegel's philosophy, according to Kierkegaard, is a fantasy; Søren, however, is only interested in the reality of living life in the here and now.

Philosophy itself is a fantasy, in fact, as all thinking is built on words. Words are metaphors and abstractions that we place between us and reality. They create a buffer that protects us from experiencing life as-it-is. Words, ideas, and thinking all mediate reality and make it palatable, because they distort reality into something we can tolerate.

Humans do this, Kierkegaard said, because reality as-it-is is horrifying; we do not want to face its implications. These horrors are our own subjective truths that we spend most of our lives running from. One of the biggest is the fact that you yourself will one day die. Another is to see yourself as living a very brief span of time, when compared with eternity. We are profoundly insignificant. And even though we may be aware of our insignificance, we run through our lives doing insignificant things, realizing that very little of what we accomplish in our lives will have any enduring value whatsoever. The problem is, once a person gets such a glimpse, he or she falls into a vertigo of meaninglessness. If nothing I do has any enduring value, why bother to get out of bed in the morning? Why not just end it all and get it over with? How can one not be crippled by despair and ennui?

Yet Søren invites us to stare bravely into the gaping maw of time, acknowledge our own finitude, and not allow such knowledge to devastate us. But how do we do this?

He finds his key in three stages of moral development that are necessary if we are to face our own finitude and not slit our wrists. The first stage is the most natural; it is the *Aesthetic* stage, typified by the literary character of Don Juan. The Aesthetic man is ruled by his passions, loves food, drink, women, and, in general, all the pleasures of the flesh. This is as far as many people go, he says, but many people will not be content with such a shallow existence.

Those people will most likely look for a standard of morality; this is the *Ethical* stage, typified by Socrates. The Ethical person is concerned with fairness, right conduct, and order, both external and internal.

This is as far as his philosophy went for a while, and he saw in these two stages a reflection of his own experiences with Regine. When he was in love with her, and under the rule of his passions, he was living the Aesthetic life. But when he realized it would be unfair to her to subject her to a life filled with his own crippling melancholy, he sacrificed his own desires for, as he thought, "her own good." This he took to be the Ethical choice, and though he felt very good about himself for being so magnanimous (albeit in a very twisted way), he was still plagued with guilt over the whole episode.

Then something else happened that added a new dimension to his philosophy. While visiting his hometown, he passed Regine while coming out of church. To his great amazement, she smiled at him, and nodded. You could have pushed him over with a feather. She didn't hate him! She did not consider him to be such a schmuck!

This caused a whirlwind of doubts and ideas in Søren's head. He decided that there was a third stage of development, the *Religious* stage, typified by Abraham. Like Abraham, Søren's own father had sacrificed his son—or at least his son's mental health—in an attempt to make him an ethical person. Likewise, Kierkegaard had sacrificed his own happiness with Regine in order to live an ethical life. But Abraham's hand was stayed at the last minute—he *didn't* kill Isaac. The truly religious person does not need to renounce the world in order to embrace the ethical; for the person of faith, both the

Aesthetic and the Ethical can be held in creative tension.

(Let's pretend for the moment that this conclusion does *not* prove Hegel's thesis/antithesis/synthesis to be true after all, shall we, since this would no doubt have enraged our mystic of the day!)

But how does one reach this Religious stage? Not by feeling, for that is the Aesthetic method; not by thinking, for that is the Ethical way. No, the only way to progress to the Religious stage is to embrace absurdity, to jump into the illogical, or as Kierkegaard says, to make a leap of faith.

Once one has stood before the gaping maw of time, has grasped his or her own insignificance, how does one go on? By making a leap of faith; by performing an essentially illogical act; by casting oneself upon the invisible arms of God, not knowing whether one will be caught or not.

Kierkegaard calls the person who can do this a "Knight of Faith." As Donald Palmer explains it, the Knight of Faith is "an individual who has looked profoundly into the world and seen that at the deepest level we are alone." The Knight of faith alone bears the consequences of his actions, he is alone with his God and must justify his actions in light of eternity. This results in a kind of divine madness, where a person can, apparently, if we are to take the Abraham story seriously, commit the most unethical acts, and yet be accountable to no one but God alone.

What is the result of this development? A person who owns his own truth; he does not borrow the truths of his society or his church or his friends. Each person must face his own essential aloneness, see through the ephemerality of the Aesthetic, realize the limitations of the Ethical, and emerge as one's own person, alone with his God, alone as he faces eternity. This is a heroic task, in Kierkegaard's view, for it insists that we cast off all of our philosophical moorings, and hold only to our own subjective truths. And not only hold to them, but embrace them, believe them, internalize them, and stand in them, strong and unafraid. It is a Herculean task, but the only one which has integrity for a person of our time.

It is the kind of hero we have adopted—just think of Bruce Willis in the *Die Hard* movies, or Captain Kirk—individuals strong enough to know when the rules do not apply to them when pursuing a greater good.

In many ways, Kierkegaard presaged much of postmodernism.

Just as postmodernism has embraced a radical relativity and eschewed the notion of knowable objective truth, Kierkegaard denied the validity of objective systems of thought and proclaimed the sovereignty of the individual. It takes great courage to be an individual, to not be swayed by society, religion, or family opinion. One must instead hold to the very little bit that each of us can actually know to be true, and that very little bit is our own subjective experience. In some ways, Kierkegaard was saying, "Have faith in yourself," but in a way that does not minimize the scariness of the world or the real dread one feels when one grasps one's own limitedness and ephemerality.

In this way, he is a great prophet for our own time, and a mystic in his own counterintuitive way. For in rejecting objective systems and in facing the unknown with courage, he invites us all to enter into a relationship with Mystery. This relationship requires a leap of faith, both in ourselves, and in the essential goodness of God's purpose. For many, his Religious stage is a cop-out; that like so many philosophers he came face to face with the difficult dilemma of one's own existence, and posited an illogical answer that is too convenient to be any actual good.

I think this is a valid criticism, but perhaps it all comes down to whether or not one is willing to consider that there may actually be more to reality than we can know. My subjective experience is all I have, yet I can imagine something beyond it, and I have the power to entrust myself to this unknown Mystery in full knowledge of the fact that I may in fact be fooling myself. This takes courage, and courage is not a thing that one necessarily is born with. It must be cultivated.

Søren never did find happiness with Regine, but he did attempt to embody the heroic philosophy that he wrote about. He died very young, at the age of 42, less than half the lifespan of his own father; and yet, in that short time, his own courage and his tenacious refusal to let go of a lost love forged in him something very rare indeed: a life of enduring value, remembered and revered long after his death. Rest eternal grant to him, O Lord, and let light perpetual shine upon him.

Jesus, you of all people know how hard it was to be a person; to have one's own ideas, and to hold fast to them in the face of fierce opposition.

Yet you did not let your fears control you, and even stared death in the face and did not blink. Give us a measure of your resolve, to face the fact of our own solitude and impending death with courage; give us a portion of your faith, that we may believe in some higher purpose though our senses deny it. This is the challenge of living in our time; help us to bear it with dignity. Amen.

⊕ Preached at Grace North Church June 30, 2002.

24 | Madame Blavatsky

In *The Wizard of Oz*, probably America's most successful indige-
nous mythology, L. Frank Baum tells of a Wizard who appears to
a small band of adventurers who had gone to seek him; namely,
the Scarecrow, the Tin Woodman, the Cowardly Lion, and little
Dorothy with her dog, Toto. The amazing thing is that in the book,
he does not appear to them at the same time, as he does in the film.
First he appeared to Dorothy as a giant, scary, disembodied head.
Then, he appeared to the Scarecrow as a beautiful young woman
with wings. To the Tin Woodman, the Wizard appeared as a terrible
beast, with the head of a rhinoceros, with five eyes, five long arms
and five long, slim legs. It was covered with thick, woolly hair. The
next morning the Great and Terrible Oz appears to the Cowardly
lion as a ball of flame.

Baum was trying to make a point in his story: great figures appear
differently to different people. What one person may see as an innocent and intriguing woman, another may see as a terrible beast,
while another may see her as the mouthpiece of disembodied wisdom. These images are not random, of course. L. Frank Baum was a
Theosophist by religion, a religion founded by one extraordinary
woman—or was she a beast?—Madame Blavatsky.

She was born in 1831, and named Helena Hahn. She was the

daughter of a Russian colonel, who by ethnicity was part of a tribe of expatriate Tibetans who had migrated to Russia and struggled as people of a minority religion in a Christian country. Her mother was the daughter of Princess Helena Dolgoroukov, and she died when our hero was only eleven. Her cousin was Sergei Witte, who would later become prime minister and personal friend of Rasputin's.

At sixteen she married middle-aged Count Nikifor Blavatsky, a famed world traveler twenty-four years her senior, mostly to prove her nurse wrong. Her nurse told her that with her mouth, she'd never get a man. So she landed a Count, and promptly left him, never consummating the marriage. After this, she appeared in Egypt with an Italian opera singer, studied voodoo in New Orleans, lived among the Indians in Canada, journeyed by wagon train to consult with the Mormons, worked as a bareback rider in a circus, taught piano in Paris and London, served as a medium, and managed an artificial flower factory. Now, this is all from her own recollections, and the degree to which this bizarre resume is based in fact is a matter of speculation. Still, it is her story, her myth, if you will, and the spirit of such a resume is certainly true, even if some of the particulars are fanciful.

In 1873, at the age of 42, she found herself once again in America, which was in the grip of a spiritualist craze. Seances were never bigger than when she came on the scene. Table rapping, levitating trumpets, and mysterious voices were all the rage, as people traveled long distances to gain a comforting word from a departed loved one. Blavatsky reveled in this occult atmosphere, and it was at one such séance that she met her platonic life partner—Colonel Henry Olcott. Colonel Olcott was Blavatsky's mirror opposite. She was a large woman, he a diminutive man; she was a loud, brash chain smoker; he was a quiet, naive man with no visible vices. Together, they formed an association that would quite literally change the world: the Theosophical Society.

The Theosophical Society was born in 1875. The word "theosophy" is not original to them, of course. For many years the word was a synonym for "mysticism" in general and was applied to the work of many mystics we have already covered, such as Meister Eckhart, Jakob Boehme, and Paracelsus. But Blavatsky and Olcott made the term their own, and it has ever since been associated with their Society. The word literally means "the wisdom of God," and it was their single-minded mission to make this wisdom available to the world.

Originally, the society had three stated goals: 1) To form a nucleus of the universal brotherhood of humanity, without distinction of race, creed, sex, caste, or color; 2) to encourage the study of comparative religion, philosophy, and science; 3) to investigate the unexplained laws of nature and the powers latent in humanity.

Now, if they had stopped there, the Society would have had long and appealing value. There is nothing in those three stated goals that I personally disagree with, and if that were all that the Theosophical Society promoted, I would probably be a Theosophist today. And indeed, many people were attracted to this initial formula.

But Blavatsky had too much of the showman in her, and her followers were fascinated with occult phenomena, which she was only too willing to provide. Soon letters began falling from the ceiling, appearing out of nowhere from one of several "Ascended Masters."

According to Theosophical mythology, the Ascended Masters were once human, but through endless cycles of reincarnation, have become enlightened beings who guide the spiritual evolution of humankind from their remote hermitages in the Himalayas. This myth took on a life of its own, especially after Blavatsky and Olcott relocated their headquarters to Adyar, India. There they found a culture predisposed to believe in gurus, even disembodied ones. And even for those in Europe and America, odd spiritual wisdom was easier to swallow when coming from alleged Ascended Masters than it was coming from a chain-smoking Russian medium.

Many notable people were attracted to Blavatsky's teachings. Journalist A.P. Sinnet was the recipient of many letters from the Ascended Masters, and he believed in them whole-heartedly. Eventually enough of the letters were produced to be published. *The Mahatma Letters* runs seven volumes, and the originals now reside in the British Museum. Yeats was also under Blavatsky's spell for a time, and Sherlock Holmes' inventor Arthur Conan Doyle was also an avid Theosophist and published regularly in Theosophical journals.

But not everyone was so enamoured. The Society for Psychical Research sent an investigator to India after hearing from Blavatsky's estranged housekeeper. The investigator was not surprised to find that the "shrine" in which the Masters' letters appeared shared a wall with Blavatsky's bedroom, and a secret panel between the two was discovered. Blavatsky went into a rage and insisted that the house-keeper's husband, a carpenter, had put the secret panel there just to discredit her.

But the faithful were not deterred. Blavatsky herself laments promulgating the Ascended Masters myth in her later letters, relieved that the investigator had simply declared her a fraud. That was better, after all, than him discovering the truth about her masters. The truth, according to one researcher, was that her masters were indeed real, but instead of enlightened, once-human beings living in remote places, they were, in fact, her real-life mentors; even the paintings of the Ascended Masters bore remarkable resemblance to the men who trained and guided her.

That she was ready to dispense with this mythology is clear in that she published a parody of the doctrine in one of the Theosophical journals, in which she herself appears as a gigantic dis-embodied head. The fact that L. Frank Baum had the great and pow-erful Oz appear to Dorothy in exactly the same way is no accident—I believe it is a direct reference to this parody. And Oz is found out by Dorothy and her companions. He is discovered to be a "hum-bug," a fraud, with no magical powers at all. Dorothy is incensed and tells him, "I think you are a very bad man!" (p. 162). But listen to his reply, "Oh, no, my dear; I'm really a very good man; but I'm a very bad Wizard, I must admit."

Perhaps the same can be said for Oz's model, Madame Blavatsky. For upon leaving India and the myth of the Ascended Masters behind, she went to Europe and composed her magnum opus, *The Secret Doctrine*. This amazing work ran over 1,500 pages, and is a very rewarding work indeed. For in it, Blavatsky proposes an evolu-tionary scheme that made Darwin's seem miniscule by comparison. She posits that we are not the products of random chance, but the recipients of a grand cosmic plan designed to lead us to greater and greater spheres of enlightenment, until the whole of the universe is aware of its own divinity.

In formulating this plan, she distills the spiritual wisdom of Hinduism, Buddhism, Sikhism, Taoism, Egypt, and the Western Mystery traditions into one great, lumbering system that is as stag-gering in its scope as it is incomprehensible. Blavatsky was thus the first of a long line of synthesizers that tried to shoehorn various reli-gious and mystical traditions into one coherent system, always with mixed results. After her, Aleister Crowley would create his own synthesis, followed by many others, all the way up to Ken Wilber in our own day.

The problem with the synthesis approach is that these are different systems and were not intended to be pasted together. But according to the synthesizers, Truth is One, and by looking at the disparate elements of many traditions, one can gain a greater grasp of the whole, of the elusive truth that every tradition points to but none can encompass. *The Secret Doctrine* attempts to encompass this Truth, certainly, but only succeeds in being an unruly mess, albeit a brilliant one indeed.

She died on May 8, 1891, from a combination of many illnesses including heart disease, kidney disease, and gout, leaving behind a legacy that would continue to snowball long after her death. The Theosophical Society would continue to swell, reaching its apex in the 1920s, with millions of members worldwide. The myth of the Ascended Masters also outlived her, and even today there are many splinter groups that still honor the mysterious enlightened men in the Himalayas. Probably the largest of these is the gun-stockpiling Church Universal and Triumphant headed by Elizabeth Clare Prophet.

Blavatsky was a remarkable woman, certainly, but in the end, can we say that she was anything other than a charlatan? I believe she was much more than that. For although she used dishonest means, and was not above publicly ridiculing people she thought were too darn naïve for their own good, she was also a prophet with a timely message, even for us today. We might even say she was a soldier, fighting a spiritual war on two fronts.

First, she fought against Christian arrogance. If we are to believe her account, she was raised in a tribe of dislocated Buddhists in a Christian country, and railed all her life against the spiritual hubris of Christianity. It was her belief that the spiritual wisdom of the East was at least as valid as the wisdom offered by Western traditions, and she spent her life exploring and explicating these ideas, making them accessible to the average person. In this she was a popularizer of great skill, and we in the West are indebted to her. For it was partly through her efforts that the first Parliament of World Religions was held in Chicago over a hundred years ago, an event that introduced Hinduism and Buddhism to America and fired the American imagination for esoteric wisdom. Her attack on Christianity would eventually come full circle, when thirty years after her death, the Theosophical Society spawned its own Christian tradition: the Liberal Catholic Church. As you probably know, St. Raphael's Liberal Catholic Church meets in this very sanctuary every Saturday morning, sporting a high Anglican-style liturgy and a very Theosophical theology.

Blavatsky's other war front was against modernism. She hated the idea that the universe could be compartmentalized and explained piece by piece. She couldn't stand the idea that science could explain away every mystery, and in her battle against this modern impulse she joined a long line of Romantics, such as Blake and Yeats, who felt that there was much more mystery in the world than could possibly be explained by science. In this particular war she had unwitting allies in the Christian fundamentalists, although I'm sure they would decline to drink from her canteen.

Her writings and the sheer force of her personality fostered a movement that rose above the petty table-rapping of the spiritualists and embraced a cosmic vision that gave hope to millions who were not being spiritually fed by their religious traditions. In doing so, she inspired artistic schools that led the way to non-representational modern art, pioneered the use of archetypes that foreshadowed depth psychology, posited layer upon layer of past civilizations which was amazingly close to modern theories of plate tectonics, and eschewed religious and scientific parochialism thus presaging the theories of Einstein and Heisenberg and the whole of post-modern relativism.

So, was Madame Blavatsky a charlatan? Probably. Was she at the same time a fearless spiritual adventurer? Most certainly, and we owe her a lot. It is safe to say that the entire New Age movement has its roots in the nineteenth-century occult revival she was so instrumental in bringing about. And whatever you may think of New Agers, the movement certainly provided those who are turned off by traditional spiritual paths a way to discover new meaning for their lives and a deeper connection to the universe than they had known before. And as shallow and silly as so many New Age groups may seem, the sincere seeker can see through the proprietary jargon to the universal truths that may be there, and keep on seeking, as one guru after another falls away.

After all, it wasn't until after the Great and Terrible Oz was revealed to be a humbug that he actually became a useful and productive person for Dorothy and her little band of adventurers. Likewise, acknowledging Madame Blavatsky's feet of clay should not dissuade us from appreciating the treasure that she also was, and continues to be, long after her death.

Lord of the Universe, you are the God of both saints and sinners, and most of us are not one or the other, but both at the same time, much like your servant, Helen Blavatsky. Help us to realize, as she taught, that truth is true wherever you find it, that no one religion—including science—has all the answers, and that we would all be a good deal better off if we took our own culture with a dose of humility, and realized that every people has been granted wisdom, and that that wisdom is not theirs alone, but belongs to the whole of the human family. Help us to have a measure of her openness to other traditions, and an ounce of her chutzpah. For we ask this in the name of the Ascended Master we know best, even Jesus Christ. Amen.

⊕ *Preached at Grace North Church July 14, 2002.*

25 | Phineas Parkhurst Quimby

Do any of you have friends that you love dearly, but sometimes you just want to brain them? Truly one of the most frustrating people I know, and one of the most beloved, is "Terry." Terry is one of these people for whom nothing ever seems to pan out. She is always out of work, never has a steady date, and is sure that someone is out to get her at all times. Yes, she's a little paranoid. Yes, she is frustrating. But every now and then she laughs this laugh that reminds me that she is more than simply a bundle of negativity, that there is a real person in there that I care about.

Unfortunately, people are so often put off by the aura of failure and despair she carries around like an umbrella that they don't stick it out long enough to see her positive qualities. I do admit, she often does her best to conceal them.

One time she was on her way to a job interview. I asked her what she thought her chances were. "Not good," she answered. "Why not?" I asked. She shrugged. Terry is well educated, very smart, and often very funny. From what I've seen of her, she is also a dependable worker. A week later I asked her if she had heard about the job. "I didn't get it," she sighed, adding, "Of course."

Not long after, Terry got some temp work. But her very first week she fell ill, and was out half the week. Of course, they fired her. Now is it just me, or do you think there may be something of the self-ful-filling prophesy-thing going on, here?

I don't feel like there's much I can do to help Terry. She kind of has to help herself. But perhaps, if our mystic of the day were around today, he might have been able to make a difference.

Phineas Parkhurst Quimby—known as "Park" to his friends—was born in Lebanon, New Hampshire in 1802, but soon moved with his family to Belfast, Maine, where he was to spend most of his life. He dropped out of school after just a couple of weeks because his family was so poor. He was soon apprenticed to a clockmaker, a craft he excelled at. At the time, clockmakers did more than simply assemble clocks. They covered some of the same ground we would assign to scientists today, and indeed, Quimby turned out to be quite a talented inventor. Four of his inventions received patents, and he was one of the first people to build daguerreotypes, a very early kind of camera.

Working on clocks was a very meditative activity for Quimby, and it impressed upon him a mystical understanding of the universe. The world was like a clock, dependable, predictable, following unmalleable laws of its own, which, if they could just be divined, could be used by humankind for their betterment and progress. This is not a surprising insight—the notion of the clock-maker God had been around for a while by this time. But building clocks provided a solid ground of experience which would later "click" or perhaps "tick" with Quimby.

Another piece of the puzzle that took a while to "click" happened when Quimby was very ill in his late 20s. At the time, his doctors informed him that his liver was affected, his kidneys were diseased, and his lungs were nearly consumed. The medicine they gave him was slowly poisoning him, and he had already lost many teeth because of it. Today, it is speculated that he was suffering from tuberculosis. Once when he was very ill a friend suggested that he take a brisk ride on a horse. Not able to simply sit still and die, Quimby decided to give his friend's cure a try. But he was too weak to ride, so he went for a carriage ride instead. Unfortunately, the horse would not cooperate, and he found himself walking in front of the buggy, leading the horse. Finally he was so exhausted, that he was just barely able to climb into the drivers' seat. There he stayed for hours, for he was simply too weak to raise the whip, even if the horse *were* cooperating.

Eventually, Quimby spied a farmer out in his field. Too weak to call for help, Quimby had to wait until the farmer had plowed around a three-acre lot before he was close enough to hear Quimby's feeble cries. When the farmer came over, Quimby asked him to start his horse for him.

What happened then is history, for as the horse started to move, Quimby says, "excitement took possession of my senses, and I drove the horse as fast as he could go, up hill and down, till I reached home and, when I got into the stable, I felt as strong as I ever did."

Quimby didn't quite know what to make of this experience, but it provided another building block in what would later become a very unique spiritual system.

When Quimby was 36, a French mesmerist named Charles Poyen, who called himself an expert in "animal magnetism," lectured in Belfast. Mesmerism posited that there was an ethereal substance between all bodies, magnetic in nature, and that healing could be effected by manipulation of this invisible force. Poyen actually effected a number of miraculous cures, and Quimby was an instant convert. He dropped everything and began following Poyen from town to town, learning not only mesmerism, but how to put on a good show as well.

He soon excelled at the technique, and teamed up with Lucius Berkmar, a talented clairvoyant, and hit the road with his own travelling healing show. The press began to take notice, as the cures were coming fast and furious. Somewhere along the way, Quimby realized that Berkmar was not diagnosing actual illnesses when he went into his clairvoyant trances, nor was he prescribing actual cures. What he was doing was discerning the patients' own beliefs about their illnesses, and addressing those alone.

Suddenly, everything clicked. The dependability of a clockwork universe spoke to Quimby of a science, a provable principle which, once understood, could be used by anybody. His horse ride and its miraculous effects suddenly made sense. How a person thinks directly and predictably affects their health.

Quimby himself said that his teaching is not new at all, but is clearly illustrated in the New Testament.

Jesus was traveling around, healing people right and left. When some blind men approached him, Jesus asked them, "Do you believe that I am able to do this?" And they answered, "Yes, Lord." So he touched their eyes, and said, "According to your faith, let it be done to you." It was not the touch that healed them, it wasn't his magic power: it was, as Jesus told them, their own faith that cured them. It was their own beliefs, their own thoughts about the disease that made the difference.

Quimby felt he had found the medical holy grail—he had discovered Jesus' own healing technique, and what's more, he could teach it to others.

Quimby posited five basic doctrines foundational to his system:

1. Happiness is determined by belief
2. Life responds to our beliefs
3. Beliefs can be changed
4. We exist within the Universal Spirit
5. Perfect wisdom/knowledge/understanding is available to us.

Accordingly, then, disease is due to false beliefs, which a person develops by impressing wrong thoughts on the mind. To eliminate disease, one must simply discover the cause, the erroneous thought that led to the disease. As Quimby himself puts it, "The trouble is in the mind, for the body is only the house for the mind to dwell in. If your mind has been deceived by some invisible enemy into a belief, you have put it into the form of a disease, with or without your knowledge. By my theory or truth I come in contact with your enemy and restore you to health and happiness" (3:208, *Complete Writings*).

Quimby dissolved his partnership with Berkmar, and set up a private practice for himself. During the course of his healing career "Dr. Quimby," as he had come to be called, estimated that he saw some 12,000 patients. Unfortunately, he was so busy seeing patients that he never took time to write his teachings down in any systematic form. But the little group of disciples that gathered at his home to be taught were much better organized, and it is because of them and their often voluminous writings that we even know of Quimby today.

The most famous of these disciples was a young woman whom Quimby had cured named Mary Baker Eddy. It was Quimby who had first coined the term "Christian Science" to describe his method, but once Mary Baker Eddy had set out on her own, she took the name for herself, and disavowed all ties to Quimby. Even today, the

Christian Science Church denies Quimby's place as the true founder
of their faith.

Mary Baker Eddy was not the only one to go forth and prosper
with Quimby's ideas. Emma Curtis Hopkins carried on his teachings, working with Eddy for a brief time, but then separating herself
from Eddy when Christian Science became too dogmatic. From
Hopkins' students sprang the larger New Thought movement which
has truly impacted the world. The groups which sprung from her
study circles include the Unity School of Christianity, the Church of
Religious Science, and Science of Mind. All of these groups cooperate through a larger umbrella organization, the New Thought
Alliance. Only Christian Science refuses to associate itself with its
sibling movements.

New Thought provided a uniquely American form of spirituality
that found great success. Nondogmatic, its followers did not eschew
doctors as Christian Scientists do, for they recognized the placebic
value of taking a pill. It was a religion that felt it held the secret to
Jesus' own methods, yet did not deify him in the same way as traditional Christian Churches. New Thought followers remained open
to spiritual influences, and found sympathetic teachings in
Emerson's Transcendentalism, the Hindu *Upanishads*, and the mystical teachings of many traditions. Perhaps the best known of
Quimby's progeny was Norman Vincent Peale, whose *Power of
Positive Thinking* popularized Quimby's teachings into a clear, practical, and very American spirituality that was non-sectarian and easily practiced by religious and non-religious folk alike.

A serious workaholic, Quimby quite literally worked himself into
an early grave. He died of exhaustion on Jan. 16, 1866 at his home
in Belfast, Maine. His epitaph stated the simple truth about him:
"Greater love hath no man than this, that a man lay down his life for
his friends." Quimby gave his life for his patients, many of whom
went on to carry this unlettered medicine-show barker's unique
Science of Mind to the nations.

There are problems with Quimby's teachings. For one thing, I
cannot accept that all disease is in the mind. This places the blame
for illness on those who are ill. For those who are seriously ill, I cannot think of a more destructive notion. Not only must they carry the
burden of illness, but they must also carry the burden of guilt—that
it is their own fault that they are sick. This is similar to many New

Age schools of thought that I find equally hard to stomach, such as the notion that people who are starving in Africa do so because they chose to in a previous life—utter rubbish.

But I do not think that all of what Quimby says is rubbish. I think a lot of it is right-on. I agree that a lot of what ails people is in their heads. I do think that a person's health is affected by how he or she thinks. Our attitude determines much about what happens in our lives.

For instance, I wish my friend Terry would see that she is not simply a sad failure, but that there is within her a fun, capable, intelligent, and responsible person who has what it takes to be successful and happy. If only she could take down the umbrella of gloom she carries with her everywhere. Sure, sometimes it is appropriate to be depressed. But on sunny days, the umbrella should go in the rack.

Divine Healer, you tell us that it is our own faith which saves us, our own faith which heals us, and we long to believe that it is so. Help us to believe in ourselves, even as you believe in us. Help us to see how our own thoughts subvert and sabotage us, and help us to change our thinking even as we change our fortunes. For you are the divine healer who leads us by example, and inspires us to have a new mind, even that mind which was in Christ Jesus. Amen.

⊕ *Preached at Grace North Church August 4, 2002.*

26 | Henri Bergson

As many of you know, my grandfather died not too long ago.
My parents lived next door to my grandparents during my
first six years. This was a hellish arrangement for my mother
and her mother-in-law, but for a little boy it was heaven to have
Grandma and Grandpa so close at hand. Although it has been a long
time since I have lived near them, I have always felt very close to my
grandparents, and it was a very sad day indeed when I heard that my
grandfather had finally succumbed to the cancer that was eating
away at him.

As the only minister in the family, I was asked to conduct the
funeral. I was honored to have been asked: my family are all Baptists
after all, and I am the renegade catholic among them, so it was very
affirming. But after much thought, I had to decline. There are a
number of reasons for this. First of all, I had my own mourning to
do—I wasn't at all certain I would be able to hold it all together long
enough to get through the service. Second, the only service I know
how to do, the prayer book service, would not have gone over very
well with my family, nor would it have appropriately honored my
Baptist grandfather, for whom the phrase "written prayers" was oxy-
moronic. Third, Grandad's death had thrust me into a bit of an existential crisis. I was very aware at the funeral that all the places had
shifted. Just last year, Grandad was the old man, my father was the

householder, and I was still the youngster. But in the twinkling of an eye that had all changed: my father was the old man, I am suddenly the middle-aged guy, and my nephew Joey is no longer a child, but a young man.

Rarely do you see such an obvious changing of the guard, and it shook me up. It shook my Dad, too. I have never before in my life seen him sob; it was a healing sight indeed, but only added to the surreality of the day.

These were the reasons I declined to do the memorial, but as I sat in the congregation during the service, another reason dawned on me that had not occurred to me before, one that seemed more important than all the others. The truth is, I could not stand up there at the podium and say the things they would have wanted me to say.

All I can say is, thank God for the *Book of Common Prayer*. In times of deep distress, it prays for us. When the heart is groaning with sighs too deep for words, the liturgy provides the words. There is something deeply human and infinitely comforting in its pages, and I truly could not do my job without it. I can proclaim, "I am the resurrection and the life, saith the Lord" from its pages, but there's no way I could stand up there at my Grandfather's funeral and tell everyone about the joys of heaven, promise them that my Grandfather is walking with Jesus, or that they would see him again. I don't know any of those things, and I can't simply stand up there and lie to people.

How can I offer people a comfort that I cannot afford myself? I'm *terrified* of death! I see my own father growing old in front of my eyes. I feel my own time slipping away from me—and I am helpless to stop it. I grasp at my days in vain. I know I will die—and I'm *scared*.

When we were born we awakened into a mystery. The universe is a vast mystery which we will never figure out. We honor our religious traditions because we need guidance, and those lights that guided others help us see one another better as well. We gather together as community because it is natural to hold hands in the dark.

I deliver sermons because I need to share my search—and my discoveries—with you. I can't give you answers—not with any integrity. I can only share my own questions.

Now, lest you get the wrong idea, this is not a negative sermon. I think life is wonderful. I also have faith that some higher purpose is being worked out. Just the fact that the death penalty is illegal in every industrialized nation in the world—except, I'm ashamed to say, our own—is evidence that we are growing beyond the law of tooth and fang. The example of Judaism shows the degree to which our religious traditions have facilitated this very growth, have given us laws, and enabled us to become more than we were.

One thing that I can be certain of is that in a very real way, my grandfather continues his life in my father and in me. The flow of life from generation to generation was laid bare before me the day of his funeral—a continuous stream of which I am both observer and participant. In some sense I am a continuation of my grandfather's project. I am part of the flow of life that began in the mists of pre-history, ran through him, and continues to run through me. I saw my family as an organism, a serpent coiling through time, which had just shed its skin.

Henri Bergson's shoulder would have been a good one to cry on that day, as I believe that, more than most folks, he would have understood what I was feeling. For Bergson likewise viewed the universe as a continuous flow of life, and he also struggled to envision a God that made sense to him, often to the consternation of his fellows.

Bergson was born in Paris in 1859, the son of a Polish Jew and an Irish mother. He was an exceedingly bright child and seemed to win every intellectual competition he entered. At 17 he won a prize for solving a mathematical puzzle reputed only to have been solved by Pascal so far, and that answer had been unpublished and so was unavailable. But Henri figured it out. As a young man, Bergson taught philosophy until, reaching middle age, his college was known as "the House of Bergson."

During this time Bergson developed the ideas that would make him the toast of Europe, and one of the most influential thinkers of the twentieth century. Bergson's project was to refute the nearly all-encompassing philosophy of determinism, the creeping scientific dogma that all things are merely the sum of their parts, that all things can be dissected and quantified, that human behavior can be reduced to a predictable pattern of behavioral mechanization.

Like the Romantics who came before him, Bergson wanted to champion intuition over intellect, free will over determinism, life over the clockwork assemblage of parts. It seemed to him that the scientist dissecting a dead frog's leg in a lab, thinking he was studying *life,* was fooling himself. There had to be a better way, and Bergson set out to find it.

He found his answer in a kind of Gnostic dualism. He saw two opposing forces in the universe: *matter,* the tendency of which is always towards rest, dissolution, and chaos; and *life,* which is dynamic, ambitious, and perpetually strives upward beyond itself. As Nikos Kazantzakis describes it, "in the temporary living organism these two streams collide: (a) the ascent toward composition, toward life, toward immortality; (b) the descent toward decomposition, toward matter, toward death. Both opposing forces are holy." These forces are always in opposition, and in some ways the entire drama of the universe can be understood as the struggle—or perhaps the dance—between them.

While science tends to separate things into parts, including time, Bergson's philosophy tends to see all things as part of a continuous flow. Time, after all, does not happen in moments. Life is not like a movie reel; a succession of snapshots; points in time are not distinct. Instead, time is experienced as duration, as a continuum. Time is not like raindrops, it is like a river. Likewise, things in the universe are not islands, everything is dependent on everything else, we are parts of one another, all part of the continuous flow of reality.

Bergson was not convinced by Darwin's theories. He did not feel that it was natural selection that governed evolution, but instead it is guided by something he called the *elan vital,* the life force in the universe. This *elan vital* constantly strives against the downward pull of matter, trying to get higher, trying to gain complexity and consciousness. This unconscious, ambitious force was the closest thing to divinity Bergson could recognize, and thus he called the world "a machine for the making of the gods."

Kazantzakasis, a true poet, renders Bergon's vision this way:

"I stoop over chaos and listen. Someone is groaning and climbing up a secret, dangerous slope. He tramples on inorganic matter, he shapes the plant and fills it. He encamps in it with his whole being....with the longing and the power to escape. He emerges a little, breathes with difficulty, chokes. He abandons to the plants as much heaviness, as much stupor and immobility as he can and, thus disburdened, leaps, with his whole being again, farther and higher still, creating the animals and encamping in their loins. He purifies himself slowly by struggling amid their bodies, and abandons to the animals as much passion, as much slavishness, as much impotence and darkness as he can. Then once more he rises slightly, a bit lighter, and rushes to escape. It is this drive toward freedom, this strife with matter, which slowly creates the head of man. And now we feel with terror that he is again struggling to escape beyond us, to cast us off with the plants and animals, and to leap farther. The moment has come—O great joy and bitterness!—when we, the vanquished, must also be cast away among the reserve troops. Behind the stream of my mind and body, behind the stream of my race and all mankind, behind the stream of plants and animals, I watch with trembling the Invisible, treading on all visible things and ascending" (*The Saviors of God*).

This is Bergson's God: blind, clawing through matter, through the relative safety of plant life, through the predictability of instinct in animals, through the precarious free will of humanity, risking all in the ascent towards the unknown. All is a continuous flow, an ongoing struggle, an episodic drama whose outcome no one can predict. We humans have a choice: we can see our part in the scheme of things and cooperate, and enable the life force to thrive, or we can resist it, aid the forces of entropy, and inhibit God in his task. Kazantzakis says we have the opportunity to be God's saviors, we can choose to save or damn him in his quest. Yes, life will use us, and cast aside our carcasses when it is finished with us, and no amount of temper tantrums on our part will change that. Life will thrive at all costs, with our consent and cooperation or without it.

Bergson gave his consent, and spent his life trying to help the rest of us fathom God's dread ascent from chaos, persuading people that they have a role to play in God's success. As France toppled in the direction of Germany during the war, Bergson was offered an exemption from the anti-Semitic laws because of his notoriety, but Bergson refused. Yet before he fell to any human enemy he succumbed to bronchitis on January 3, 1941. His body fell beneath the feet of his God, yet his memory endures and continues to inspire, long after his death.

I thought a lot about death in preparing this sermon. About my own death and about my grandfather's. My family is a continuous flow of life in which I am a but a chapter, a chapter that will close and succeed to another in the blink of an eye. Yes, I am terrified, but I am also comforted. It is a story I am honored to have had a part in.

The life of this community is also a continuous flow, a microcosm of the universe, in a way. There is a spirit attempting something grand here. I have no children and will not be able to continue my grandfather's project in a biological sense. But I give birth in other ways. This parish is my family, too, and I have become a part of its history. My choices, my presence, even my sermons contribute to the reality that is unfolding in our community, as intuition seeks to guide it to be something greater than it is. I think of the many folks who have passed on before us: Ed Vanek, the Azers, Professor DeVelbiss, Harvey, and now Laura. They are gone, and yet, they are not gone. In a very real way, we stand on their shoulders; the project they began, we continue. The vision they held is carried firmly and resolutely in our hands. Their death is not the end, but simply the turning of a wheel much greater than they ever were as individuals. It is the wheel of the world, it is the irrepressible impulse of Life, it is the engine and the incubation of God. Blessed be the name of the Lord.

O Lord, beneath your heavy feet I hear all living things being trampled on and crushed. Your face is without laughter, dark and silent, beyond joy and sorrow, beyond hope. Are you our God? Lord, you growl like a wild beast! Your feet are covered with blood, your hands are covered with mire, your jaws are heavy millstones that grind slowly. You clutch at trees and animals, you tread on human beings, you shout. You climb up the endless black precipice of death, and you tremble. Where are you going? You weep, you hook onto us, you feed on our blood, you grow huge and strong, and then you kick at our hearts. We cannot fathom you, and yet, with your servant, Henri Bergson, help us to help you, to what small degree we can. For you are working out a dread and mighty purpose, even if its end is invisible to us, even if it is invisible to you. Amen.
　　—Adapted from The Saviors of God *by Nikos Kazantzakis.*

⊕ *Preached at Grace North Church August 11, 2002.*

27 | Alfred North Whitehead

Allow me to pose a hypothetical situation: you are hiking along a mountain trail. Suddenly, you hear a muffled cry. Rushing toward the sound to investigate, you come to a cliff. About two feet down from the precipice, you see a man holding on to a root for dear life. Unfortunately the root is starting to give way, and the man's shouts are now wild and panicked. It is a long way down. The man is relieved to see you peeking over the top of the precipice and entreats you to help him. It looks to you like the root will hold a little longer, so you sit down cross-legged by the edge and think a minute.

What will you do? Will you sit there and watch him until he falls? Or will you lay flat, reach your arm down and help him up? Perhaps you should find a strong stick you could reach down to him. So many options. So little time. What will you do? I mean, just because you *can* help him, does that mean you *ought* to? The man did get down there by himself, didn't he? Why is it your job to get him out? On the other hand, if it was you, you'd want someone to help you up, wouldn't you?

That root is still holding, so you have the luxury of thinking about this some more. Are you morally obligated to help the man up? If you decide not to help him, and he falls, are you guilty of anything? What would your mother say about this? Better yet, "what would Jesus do?"

Well, by the logic of the theology we have inherited here in the West, Jesus would probably let him fall. Actually, it happens every day. Every single day tragedy strikes somewhere on this planet. Every day the news tells us of someone who falls from a cliff, about innocent people who are shot or bombed, or about planes that crash for mysterious reasons.

The hard part of this for people of faith is this: if God is all-powerful, if God is all-good and loving, why does God allow such things to happen? Why does God not reach down and intercede? If God is such a savior, how come God seems to be so dreadfully remiss at saving people? Sometimes it seems like the world is hanging by a fragile root, while God sits cross-legged at the top, watching it happen, but not caring enough to lend a hand.

Our patience for this kind of theology was sorely tested last year at this time. It is nearly one year since the terrorist attacks on September 11, and once again we are reminded of how precarious and precious human life is, how senseless the tragedy, and how criminal a God who stands by and just watches it happen.

If it were I sitting by that ledge, watching that man plummet to his death, I think I would have trouble living with myself after that. I'm pretty sure I would even be a candidate for prosecution. Even the state recognizes that gross indifference to the suffering or danger of another is a crime. And yet we whistle a tune and excuse God for the very same criminal acts—not just once, but perpetually. God, it seems, has an eternally valid "Get Out of Jail Free" card, and uses it every day.

How come no one has called him on this? How come we don't see it until something terrible happens? At that point, we are simply shaking our fists at the sky like King Lear. The storm is raging, but no one seems to be home.

It is just this sort of logical dilemma—and many others—that our mystic for the day sought to address. Alfred North Whitehead was born in England, in Ramsgate, Kent, in 1861. That was the same year that Prince Albert died. Many American young men were dying, too, as the Civil War was raging on in its second year. Darwin's *Origin of Species* had just been published, and the world was still reeling from the implications.

Alfred's childhood was full of theology: his father was an Anglican priest, and his brother Henry became a bishop in India. Their home was frequently visited by Archibald Campbell Tait, the Archbishop of Canterbury, for whom young Alfred held much admiration. Whitehead later wrote of him, "To have seen Tait was worth shelves of volumes of medieval history. He was the last of a line of great English ecclesiastics that stretched from St. Augustine of Canterbury, through Anselm, Cranmer, and Laud, to the days of Tait himself. For these men, the Church was the nation rising to the height of its civilization. They were men with vision—wide, subtle, magnificent. They failed."

Whitehead would be determined not to fail where so many divines before him had, but it was not to be for quite some time. He had a classical education and seems to have been quite a bruiser when it came to rugby. He passed his exams with such dramatic grades that Cambridge offered him a scholarship in either the classics or mathematics. His father seemed to favor mathematics, and young Alfred did not dissent. In 1884 he was invited to be part of an exclusive clique of students known as the Apostles, a group which had included Tennyson before him, and Bertrand Russell after him.

Religiously, Whitehead was profoundly influenced by the conversion of Cardinal Newman to Roman Catholicism, and nearly made the switch himself. Instead, he married Catholic. Whitehead proposed to Evelyn Wade in a smuggler's cave underneath Alfred's father's vicarage. Far from being upset that young Alfred was marrying a Catholic, his father was relieved. He was terrified that the contemplative mathematician would run off and join the Trappists or something. At least Evelyn would keep him in the real world, Catholic or no. Evelyn was the mirror opposite of the quiet, shy academician she married. She was the daughter of an army officer who spoke her mind and once had to be restrained for horsewhipping a man.

Apparently, Alfred was able to stay on her good side, and they appeared by all accounts to have had a happy, if eccentric life. In times of stress Evelyn would have fainting swoons, while Alfred used to go catatonic and mutter self-deprecating mantras under his breath while staring off into space. Still, together they read through the Apostolic Fathers, the histories of the Church Councils, the works of

Thomas Aquinas, Thomas Hooker, and many other theologians, ancient and modern. The end result of this was not an eventual conversion to Rome, but in fact, Whitehead's abandonment of religion altogether, at least for the time being.

Whitehead's professional life was going very well indeed. He and Bertrand Russell collaborated on a four-volume work on mathematics which revealed that two thousand years of mathematics were built on a faulty foundation. His fame spread, and he soon moved to London to be a freelance professor.

Not long after, disaster struck. Alfred and Evelyn's youngest son was killed in the Great War. Whitehead was grief-stricken, and his pain forced him to confront the big religious questions he had been avoiding. This led him into philosophy. In 1924 he was invited to teach philosophy at Harvard. This is ironic, as Whitehead was a mathematician who had never studied philosophy. In fact, the president of Harvard college once remarked to him, "The first lecture in a course on philosophy which you had ever attended was the one given by yourself."

And so it was that a mystically-minded mathematician entered the field of philosophy and changed the world forever. For like the best of philosophers, Whitehead was not satisfied with the answers that had been posited before him. The worldview he developed was radically the different from the one we are used to in many respects. He rejected the scientific determinism of his peers, as well as the theists' clockwork universe. He rejected the view of the church that insisted that God was all good and all powerful at the same time— after all, he had known the pain of losing a child, he was not going to fall for that one. He even rejected what our senses tell us at the most basic level. He rejected the notion that *things* are real.

Instead, he put forth the radical idea that there are only actions in the universe. There are no things acting, there are only actions that appear to be things. The universe is not a thing, not an object, but an *event*, a process moving through time. Quantum mechanics bears this out. When we get to the subatomic level, there are no things, no solid objects at all; only energy leaping in and out of existence.

Since the universe is only one big event, what does that make us? Little events, of course. I am not a man, I am an event, never to be repeated in the history of the world. I am, in Whitehead's words, an occasion. We are all occasions. My dog is an occasion, just as surely as this church service or your anniversary is an occasion. We do not live in space, we live in time. We are not creatures, but happenings.

This makes Whitehead's philosophy very difficult to talk about because our language is noun-based. We talk of "things" and what they are doing. Whitehead insists that there are no things, only events experiencing other events. There are only two languages I know of that are appropriate to this task: Hebrew and Hopi, both of which are verb-based languages, in which events are "doing," but as far as I know no one is actually writing on process thought in either language.

Realizing he was stuck with English, Whitehead created a complex vocabulary with which to describe his universe. I will try to avoid going into these terms, so please bear with me as I occasionally slip into noun-based terminology.

As in Hegel's thought, Whitehead's universe can only be taken as a whole; as Hegel said, "only the whole is real." Thus the entire universe is one huge event, like an enormous organism of which we are only parts. See? We have already slipped back into noun-based language. I'll try again. The universe is one huge happening, and we are smaller happenings, or occasions. Every occasion, from humans to rocks, has free will, and makes choices appropriate to its ability to choose and the options available to it.

God is also an event, the only event, in fact, that does not perish and succeed to another. In Whitehead's conception, God is bipolar. Don't break out the Lithium just yet—what I mean by this is that God has two distinct natures that are polar opposites. First, God has a transcendent pole, which Whitehead called God's *primordial nature*. In God's primordial nature resides the complete memory of everything that has ever happened. God's primordial nature is often likened to Plato's world of forms or Jung's collective unconscious; it is the repository of undifferentiated potentiality. Every idea that anyone has ever had, every creative leap, every imaginative possibility lives in God's primordial nature.

God also has an immanent pole, what Whitehead calls God's *consequent nature*. This is the phenomenal universe that we experience sensually. It is the event which we are all participating in, and in which the events of our own lives are played out. Now here's the neat thing: every occasion participating in God's consequent nature has full access to all the information contained in God's primordial nature at all times. It comes to us in moments of inspiration, when we are creating art or meditating. It leaps out when we dream, and whispers to us in every moment of every day. It is the "still small voice" of scripture. It is the voice of God, and it is never silent.

And it is because of this that we can say that God is powerful. For in Whitehead's universe, every occasion has free will and makes its own decisions. God has no physical hands and so cannot reach out and change anything in the world. There is no mechanism set up by which God can manipulate the world. God is powerless in this sense. God simply cannot pluck a falling plane from the sky. God cannot stop a child from falling into a well. God cannot stop anyone from doing anything evil. God simply does not have that kind of power.

So in what sense does Whitehead say God is powerful? While it is true that God does not have the power to reach out and stop things from happening, God does have the ear of every occasion in existence. God has the power to whisper to every event, big or small, at the same time. God is the ultimate world wide web, a communication portal open not just potentially to everyone at a computer, but actually, to every being, wherever they are, at all times. God can communicate simultaneously with every being in the universe: now that, my friends, is power. But it is a very limited power, for while God can persuade, God cannot coerce. Every occasion is still free to choose. We can listen to God's whisper, or we can choose to ignore it.

Just as previous generations mirrored their understanding of God in their governments, we can see how Whitehead's universe mirrors democracy well, and especially the polity in our own parish. In medieval times, the King was the ultimate authority in the land. Thus the head of the church was a "shadow" ruler, operating like a king of God's "spiritual" kingdom. In a democracy we see God not as a king, but as a companion, a co-worker in the project of the world. In our own parish, we mirror Whitehead's model to an even greater extent. Just as God has voice but no power to coerce, so the clergy in this parish have voice but no vote. This does not mean the clergy have no power in this parish. We have the power to persuade, which is a very great power indeed.

So, what is the purpose of such a God? What is the purpose of such a universe? What are we here for? How are we to live our lives? Whitehead's God is, you might say, the ultimate Epicurean. The purpose of the universe is this: intensity of feeling. God wants experience, God wants enjoyment, God wants satisfaction of God's desires, and God only gets that when *we* experience, enjoy, and are satisfied. God is only interested in feeling and in novelty of experience.

Thus, in Whitehead's universe, novelty is the greatest virtue, piety is identical with creativity, holiness is the courage to try new things, and sin is being stuck in the same old rut. God wants new experiences, diversity, and intensity. So long as we cling to safety, to tradition, and to fear, we are of little use to God, who encourages us to break out of every box we have ever known and create something new for God to delight in. God is a novelty junkie—it is our job to create and delight him, and hopefully, to take a similar delight in our own creativity and the intensity of new experiences.

This theology sounds like heaven to creative people, and is highly suspect to people who like their bed turned down on the same side every night. As a person of the creative persuasion myself, I am very attracted to Whitehead's thought. It is, in fact, the closest thing to a workable system I have ever encountered. If Whitehead is not right, he has got to be damn close, or I'll eat my *yarmulke*.

Whitehead worked on his system for many years, much to the consternation of his fellows in mathematics and philosophy, who thought he had flipped his lid with all this God-talk. Yet far from going crazy, he formulated a theology that would soon be taught at every seminary in the world. There is hardly a clergy person anywhere who is not schooled in Whitehead's thought, even if they do not accept it.

Whitehead himself laid down his speculative theology just as quickly as he took it up. He had done the work he set out to do, and he moved on to other projects. He retired at the age of 76, and in 1945 he was awarded the British Order of Merit for his efforts. Two years later, at the ripe old age of 86, his event came to an end.

The greatest advantage to Whiteheads' system is that it solves the biggest problem in the entire history of philosophy and theology: how can a loving God allow evil to happen? Simple. God is powerless to stop it. He is as heart-broken over it all as we are. Whitehead called God "the fellow sufferer who understands." This answer is amazingly congruent with scripture. After all, God did not prevent Shadrak, Meshak, and Abednigo from entering the fiery furnace. Instead, he went in there with them. He was the "fourth man in the fire" comforting them and supporting them through their trial.

Whitehead's God is as grief-stricken as we all are over the events of September 11. No doubt he was whispering as loud and strong as he could to the terrorists, but they were free events, and they apparently chose not to hear. Whitehead's God sits cross-legged by the edge of the cliff. He does not have any hands, so he cannot reach out and help the endangered man up. But he can say, "Hey, there's a rock to your right that will bear your weight," and help the person out that way; which, in fact, can be very helpful indeed. I think most of us have had the experience of vital information coming to us from a mysterious source just when we need it most. Next time that happens, thank Whitehead's God. He'd tip his hat right back at you, if he had one.

Powerful and loving God, you whisper to us in every moment of our lives. You communicate love and peace and spur us to creativity with every breath, and you entreat us to break out of our habits and the illusory safety we surround ourselves with. Give us courage to create new universes that had never been imagined before, even as your servant, Alfred North Whitehead, did. For we ask this in the name of one whose creativity shook the world, and whose field of force extends through time, and shakes us even now, even Jesus Christ. Amen.

⊕ *Preached at Grace North Church September 22, 2002.*

28 | Teilhard de Chardin

Transpersonal theorist Jean Houston, in her book *Godseed: The Journey of Christ* relates a wonderful story about when she was a little girl in New York City. One day she was late for school, and was running pell-mell through Central Park—and ran right into an old man, knocking the wind out of him. He asked her if she planned to run through her whole life that way. "It looks that way," she replied breathlessly. "Well, then *bon voyage*," the old man replied. Soon she ran into the old man again, less violently this time, and soon they were strolling together in the Park twice a week.

Young Jean was intrigued by this funny old man, for he wasn't like anyone she had ever met before. He seemed to have no self-consciousness at all, and took great delight in the smallest things, sometimes even being paralyzed in awe of them. One time she says he suddenly fell on his knees, exclaiming, "Jeanne, look at the caterpillar. Ahhh! How beautiful it is, this little green being with its wonderful funny little feet. Exquisite! Little furry body, little green feet on the road to metamorphosis. Jeanne, can you feel yourself to be a caterpillar?" "Oh, yes," she replied. "Then think of your own metamorphosis. What will you be when you become a butterfly, eh? What is the butterfly of Jeanne?"

Another time he stopped and sniffed the wind. "Jeanne, sniff the wind," he told her. "That same wind may once have been sniffed by Jesus Christ (sniff), by Alexander the Great, (sniff) by Napoleon, (sniff) by Voltaire (sniff), by Marie Antoinette!" Jean Houston comments that there certainly seemed to be a lot of French people in the air that day. "Now sniff this next gust of wind in very deeply for it contains Jeanne d'Arc! Sniff the wind once sniffed by Jeanne d'Arc. Be filled with the winds of history."

Houston says that her old man talked to dirt, and when *he* did it, it didn't seem odd or unusual. In fact it seemed like for this singular old man, conversation with rocks and soil was the most natural thing on earth. Young Jean was never able to pronounce his name. She just called him "Mr. Tayer."

We know him today as Teilhard de Chardin, and he is no less fascinating as a figure of history than he was to young Jean Houston. He was a mass of contradictions, a priest and a scientist, a devout Catholic and a suspected heretic. He had an amazing intellect, and yet a burning passion for Christ. For most of us the way of devotion and the way of knowledge are separate spiritual paths; the Hindu tradition honors both as valid ways to God, but usually a person will choose one over another according to his or her constitution. Teilhard was one of those rare creatures in whom these two paths were one and the same.

His Christian name was Pierre, and he was born at Sarcenat, France on the first of May, 1881. He was the fourth of eleven children. Family life always meant a great deal to him. His father took him on long walks in the French countryside, and instilled in him a deep and abiding love for the natural world.

He went to the Jesuit college at Villefranche, where he was a decent, but not an exceptional student. Having finished his studies, he entered the Jesuit order. Not long after that, religious orders were expelled from France. But he continued his studies abroad and began publishing in the scientific journals. He became a respected geologist and was later ordained to the priesthood.

His career as a scientist was put on hold during the great War. He spent four years as a stretcher bearer on the front lines, retrieving the wounded from the battlefield, and for his bravery he was awarded the Military Medal and the Legion of Honor. After the war, he returned to his studies and earned his doctorate. Rather unwillingly, he accepted a post as professor of geology at the Institut Catholique in Paris in 1922 and caused quite a flurry amongst his students with some of his ideas.

Much to his delight and surprise, however, he was called upon to travel to China to assist another Jesuit scientist. He enjoyed the work there and became deeply enamoured of China and the far East in general. He returned briefly to Paris to discover that some of his letters and other writings on his theory of the universe had raised quite a local ruckus. His superiors afterwards forbade him to teach or to publish. A devout and loyal Jesuit, he took his vows of obedience seriously, and feeling deeply wounded and misunderstood, he took refuge once again in his research in China. He met with great success as a paleontologist in the East and is probably most well known in scientific circles for his discovery of "Peking Man," one of the most ancient human remains yet discovered.

So just what were these ideas that his superiors found so threatening, so dangerous, that he was effectively silenced? They were very similar to the ideas we have already encountered in Bergson and Whitehead. But while Bergson's God was a blind force gnashing its way through nature, and Whitehead's God is vulnerable and time-bound, Teilhard's cosmic vision unifies matter and spirit, time and eternity, past, present, and future.

"Evolution" is the basis for Teilhard's entire cosmology. Not, as Darwinian evolution would have it, however, a random product, or the "survival of the fittest," but an evolution planned and guided by divine agency. "The magic word 'evolution' which haunted my thoughts like a tune," he writes, "was to me like unsatisfied hunger, like a promise held out to me, like a summons to be answered." Teilhard's universe is one of continuous and interwoven evolutionary threads, incorporating plants, animals, the planet, the cosmos and, most peculiar to him, not merely the physical and mental evolution of humankind, but our spiritual ascent as well.

The evolutionary ascent of human beings occurs, according to Teilhard's theory, in two stages of what he calls "planetization." The first stage is the "Go forth and multiply" stage, in which humanity expanded, both in the number of persons on the earth, and in the quality of our psychological and spiritual development.

We have now reached the end of the expanding, or "diversity" stage, and are now entering the contracting, or "unifying" stage. At this point, Teilhard's theory runs completely counter to Darwin's in that the success of humanity's evolution in the second stage will not be determined by "survival of the fittest," but by our own capacity to converge and unify. The most important initial evolutionary leap of the convergence stage is the formation of what Teilhard termed "the Noosphere."

"The idea," writes Teilhard, "is that of the Earth not only covered by myriads of grains of thought, but enclosed in a single thinking envelope so as to form a single vast grain of thought on the sidereal scale, the plurality of individual reflections grouping themselves together and reinforcing one another in the act of a single unanimous reflection." One hesitates to invoke the terms "group-mind" or "hive mentality," but they are perhaps leaps made by far less developed creatures than we that presage our own ascent. We know that such a thing can and does exist in a variety of species, especially ants, migratory birds, and others. We also know the evidence regarding the "hundredth monkey" theory, which states that once a learned behavior is taught to a significant portion of a population—in this famous example, of monkeys—the behavior becomes instinctual even for those completely isolated from the community which acquired the behavior. And C.G. Jung has certainly argued persuasively for the existence of an already operative "collective unconscious." Teilhard, then, speaks of the "collective conscious."

Teilhard waxes poetic (as he often does) when he describes it: "Noosphere...the living membrane which is stretched like a film over the lustrous surface of the star which holds us. An ultimate envelope taking on its own individuality and gradually detaching itself like a luminous aura. This envelope was not only conscious, but thinking...the Very Soul of the Earth."

The Noosphere is a fascinating and intriguing idea, one that many of us desperately want, on some level, to be true. But as we have been describing it thus far, it seems little more than science fiction. How is it that such an awesome phenomenon could possibly come to be? Amazingly, Teilhard predicts the evolution of a machine that hardly even existed in his time beyond being a glorified abacus: the computer. "Here I am thinking," he writes in *Man's Place in Nature*, "of those astonishing electronic machines by which our mental capacity to calculate and combine is reinforced and multiplied by a process and to a degree that herald as astonishing advances in this direction as those that optical science has already produced for our power of vision." Teilhard's vision of what computers would do for us is that they would, first, complete our brains, in that in the instantaneous retrieval of information around the globe what one person lacks is immediately provided by another, and second, they will improve our brains, by facilitating processes more quickly than our own resources can achieve them.

But let's come back to earth for a moment. Tielhard is keenly aware that we are identical with the material stuff of this planet, that, physically, we *are* this planet. But he goes further: not only are our bodies the stuff of the Earth's body, but our minds are the consciousness of this being, the Earth. We have supposed that we are individuals, yet we "are dust, and to dust ye shall return." We have supposed our minds are our own; but perhaps, as Jung and Teilhard suggest, we are mistaken. Teilhard, in fact, argues that it must be so, that "what we are aware of is only the nucleus which is ourselves. The interaction of souls would be incomprehensible if some 'aura' did not extend from one to the other, something proper to each one and common to all." Teilhard believes, too, that this consciousness is not only psychological, but of the greatest spiritual importance, as well. "Nothing is precious," he says, "Except that part of you which is in other people, and that part of others which is in you. Up there, on high, everything is one."

Teilhard believes that the world is "fundamentally and initially living," that the whole of cosmic history is one vast operation of evolution, culminating in a "slow but progressive concentration of a diffuse consciousness." It is especially important to note that, once we are aware of what is happening to us we can stop "groping about" in the dark and take conscious control of our evolution to speed it on its way. We can become the willing "co-creators" with God, fulfilling the birthright implied in our being made in God's image.

This is the process of "Noogenesis," or building the Noosphere, the hive mind, if you will, which will eventually become conscious of itself, and develop a super-consciousness that will posses a "personality" all its own. This is the cusp of our next great evolutionary leap, for not only do we have an evolutionary direction, Teilhard perceives that we have an end-point, a destination at which we will eventually arrive.

It is from Jesus' statement in the Apocalypse of St. John, "I am the Alpha and Omega, the beginning and the end," (Rev. 1:8) that

Teilhard obtains the name for his most important theory, that of the "Omega point." Teilhard speaks of "Omega" in two ways: as something yet to be realized, at the endpoint of evolution, yet also as a force already operative in the now and responsible for guiding the process.

This is where Teilhard's Christology enters the picture. Christ, as the Incarnation, at once human and divine, is himself the endpoint of evolution. It is within the symbolism of the risen Jesus of Nazareth from history, the first coming of Christ, that we perceive our destiny, our own resurrection. The Omega point is the second coming of Christ. In Omega all of humankind enters the state of divinity. The Incarnation event becomes the ultimate loving and creative process for Teilhard. The current of love surges from the person of the historic Christ, who had to enter into the process of physical evolution as an element in order to be the center of its convergence at the end point, Omega. As Christ inserts himself into time and space in our universe, all created matter becomes transformed and is incorporated into him.

This sounds frighteningly radical, but a strong case can be made for the orthodoxy of Teilhard's theories, especially when examining the theology of the Eastern Orthodox, who speak of the goal of the Gospel being the eventual divinization, not only of humankind, but of the universe itself. St. Athanasius in his creed speaks of Christ as one who fulfills his mission "not by conversion of the Godhead into flesh, but by taking of the Manhood into God." "To sum up," Teilhard writes, "Cosmogenesis reveals itself along the line of its main axis, first as Biogenesis, and then Noogenesis, and finally culminates in Christogenesis."

Very like the gods of Hegel, Bergson, and Whitehead, then, Teilhard's God is "bound up with" the process of evolution. Teilhard could not, even from the beginning, feel comfortable with the world-hating duality that he inherited from the Christian tradition, which placed God above and beyond the reach of the world. For him, "there is a communion with God and a communion with the Earth, and a communion with God through the Earth." Teilhard is insisting on a new sort of faith; one that incorporates "the sense of the Earth opening and exploding upwards into God; and the sense of God taking root and finding nourishment downwards into the Earth." Teilhard is not only promising the traditional escape upward, toward some celestial paradise, but just as importantly promising an escape forward, toward an evolutionary liberation. This faith holds these two not in opposition, but as complementary to one another.

We are, therefore, at the threshold of another great leap in evolution, the contraction and unification, the construction of the Noosphere, the focusing of our psychic energies into Christogenesis, aided and guided by the Holy Spirit. "The powers that we have released," Teilhard states in *Human Energy*, "could not possibly be absorbed by the narrow system of individual or national units which the architects of the human Earth have hitherto used. The age of nations has passed. Now unless we wish to perish we must shake off our old prejudices and build the Earth."

This wisdom is particularly poignant to us today as we teeter on the brink of what may very well escalate into another world war. How long can we possibly survive so long as we see ourselves in terms of "us" and "them" when the Earth is now so small? In truth, there is only "us." There is no "them." There is only the organism of the earth, and we are parts of it, instrumental to its evolution, and we have the power to impede its progress or to assist it. God's will for us is that we throw off the outdated clothes of nationalism, embrace our brothers as our very selves, and as Teilhard says, "build the earth."

Jean Houston remembers that it was on a Thursday before Easter Sunday that she last saw "Mr. Tayer." She had brought him a snail shell. His face lit up with delight. "Ah, escargot!" he exclaimed, and then shot off on an ecstatic monologue that lasted nearly an hour. He spoke of "snail shells and galaxies, the convolutions in the brain, the whorl of flowers, and the meanderings of rivers." When he had finished, she says, his voice dropped and he whispered, almost in prayer, "Omega, omega, omega." Finally he looked up. "Au revoir, Jeanne."

Jean came to meet him the Tuesday after Easter, but he was not there. Pierre Tielhard died as he wished to die, on Easter Sunday. To die on the day of resurrection was just one more contradiction so indicative of this amazing man, who saw no contradiction between science and religion. They were, in fact, to him, one and the same.

Though he was obedient to his superiors the whole of his life, there was a part of him that could not allow the total intellectual crucifixion of his vision. Before he died he entrusted his many books and papers to friends. He never saw a single one of his books published. Few in theological circles knew his name when he died. But of course, they would. After his death, he friends saw to it that his books were published. There was, after all, nothing that the Catholic church could do about it. They could not excommunicate him posthumously, although I'm sure they would have liked to. For Teilhard's vision caught on in the 1960s and '70s, utterly transforming Catholic cosmology, ending the bitter feud between science and religion in Catholic academia, and inspiring millions toward a unified field of matter and spirit.

God of the fireball at Creation, God of the Omega point, our final end, help us, with the aid of thy servant, Pierre Teilhard de Chardin, to perceive you in all we see around us; in the dirt, in caterpillars, in the faces of our friends, and especially, in the faces of our enemies. As our planet grows together, inspire us towards cooperation and love. Help us to help you in the great enterprise of the universe, the evolution of knowing and being, the end of which we can scarcely imagine. For in you is our hope, and our sure end. For we ask this in the name of him who is Alpha and Omega, beginning and end, in whom we live and move and have our being, even Jesus Christ. Amen.

⊕ *Preached at Grace North Church October 13, 2002.*

Bibliography

Abelard, Peter & Heloise. *The Letters of Abelard and Heloise*. NY: Penguin, 1974.

Backhouse, Halcyon. *The Best of Meister Eckhart*. NY: Crossroad, 1993.

Christie-Murray, David. *A History of Heresy*. New York: Oxford University Press, 1976.

Conn, Eileen and James Stewart. *Visions of Creation*. Alresford, UK: Godsfield Press, 1995. Copleston, Frederick Charles, SJ. *A History of Philosophy*, Vols. I-9. New York: Doubleday, 1944-1952

Corbishley, Thomas. *The Spirituality of Teilhard de Chardin*. NY: Paulist Press, 1971.

De Mirabilibus Mundi webpage: http://www.granta.demon.co.uk/arsm/jg/p-index.html.

Doyle, Brendan. *Meditations with Julian of Norwich*. Santa Fe, NM: Bear & Co., 1983.

Durant, William. *The Story of Philosophy*. New York: Simon & Schuster, 1922.

Edwards, David L. *Christianity: The First Two Thousand Years.* Maryknoll, NY: Orbis Books, 1997.

Fabian, Richard. *Worship at Saint Gregory's.* San Francisco: All Saints' Company, 1995.

Gallagher, Blanche. *Meditations with Teilhard de Chardin.* Santa Fe, NM: Bear & Co., 1988.

Sharman, Cecil W. *George Fox & the Quakers.* London: Quaker Home Service, 1991.

Julian of Norwich. *Revelations of Divine Love.* NY: Penguin, 1966.

Kazantzakis, Nikos. *The Saviors of God: Spiritual Exercises.* Kimon Friar, trans. (New York: Simon & Schuster, 1960), p. 12.

Layton, Bentley. *The Gnostic Scriptures.* NY: Doubleday, 1987.

Lüdemann, Gerd. Heretics: *The Other Side of Early Christianity.* Louisville, KY: Westminster John Knox Press, 1995.

Mellert, Robert B. *What is Process Theology?* NY: Paulist Press, 1975.

Palmer, Donald. *Looking at Philosophy.* Mountain View, CA: Mayfield Publishing, 1994.

Palmer, Martin. *Living Christianity.* Rockport, MA: Element Books, 1993.

Jacobi, Jolande, ed. *Paracelsus: Selected Writings.* Princeton, NJ: Princeton University Press, 1951.

Russell, Bertrand. *A History of Western Philosophy.* New York: Simon and Schuster, 1945.

Swedenborg, Emanuel. *A Compendium of the Theological Writings of Emanuel Swedenborg.* Samuel M. Warren, ed. NY: Swedenborg Foundation, 1875.

Synnestvedt, Sig. *The Essential Swedenborg.* NY: Swedenborg Foundation, 1970.

Trigg, Joseph W. *Origen.* NY: Routledge, 1998.

Trobridge, George. *Swedenborg: Life and Teaching.* NY: Swedenborg Foundation, 1992.

Van de Weyer, Robert. *The Call to Heresy.* London, UK: Lamp Press, 1989.

Wilson, Colin. *The Occult: A History.* NY: Random House, 1971.

Printed in the United States
54468LVS00001B/493-531